LEAVE YOUR LEARNING AT THE DOOR

THE WAY OF

NO THINKING

THE PROPHECIES OF JAPAN'S KUNIHIRO YAMATE

ROBERT ENGLER AND YURIKO HAYASHI

COUNCIL OAK BOOKS TULSA, OKLAHOMA

Council Oak Books

Tulsa, OK 74120

00 99 98 97 96 95   7 6 5 4 3 2 1

Book and cover design by Carol Stanton

ISBN #1-57178-008-4

Library of Congress Cataloging-in-Publication Data

Engler, Robert (Robert C.), 1936-
        The way of no thinking : the prophecies of Japan's Kunihiro Yamate
    / Robert Engler and Yuriko Hayashi.
        p.   cm.
      ISBN 1-57178-008-4 (pbk.)
      1. Decision-making—Japan.   2. Yamate, Kunihiro—Views on
    economics.   3. Yamate, Kunihiro—Political and social views.
    I. Hayashi, Yuriko, 1924- II. Title.
    HD30.23.E52   1995
    302—dc20   95-13725
                                                  CIP

WE DEDICATE

THIS BOO**K**

TO THE MEMORY OF AN

UNFORGETTABLE CHARACTER

IN OUR PLAY OF LIFE

N
O
R
I

WITHOUT WHOSE

UNCONDITIONAL HELP

THIS BOOK

WOULD NOT HAVE

BEEN POSSIBLE.

C o n t e n t s

— Acknowledgments   8

— Meeting Yamate.   10

— A Word on Thought   16

I.   The End of an Evolutionary Era   19

2.   Signs, Portents and Clues   28

3.   The Way Ahead   39

4.   Birth of the Live-Net   41

5.   Feedback from the Cosmic Shoe Store   49

6.   During the Transition to Live-Net   62

7.   Generation Gaps   72

8.   Managing the Gaps : Metadreaming   80

9.   The Limitations of Science   93

10.   A Cosmic Anatomy Class : Ectoplasms and Our Role as Catalysts   103

11.   Airplanes, Parachutes and Genies : Myths and Other Evidence for Ectoplasms   113

12.   Mosaics and the Idea of Mine: Evidence from Behavior that We Are Catalysts   120

C o n t e n t s

13.	The Curtain Comes Down : The End of the Catalyst Role	134
14.	Toward a Total Entrustment Society	143
15.	After Money, What?	152
16.	Reviews of Our Long-running Sitcoms	163
17.	Ontology: A New Focus	171
18.	Blocks to Full Consciousness : Thinking and Trying	178
19.	Our Hang-Up on Material Reality	192
20.	The Ultimate Questions	203
21.	Accessing Full Consciousness : The Way of No Thinking	220
22.	What Is Full Consciousness Like?	229
23.	Surprise! There Are No Others	239
24.	Correcting the Cosmic Hologram	253
25.	Life in the 21st Century	266
26.	The "New" Children	280
27.	Going Back on Cosmic Cruise Control	296
—	Afterword	315

Acknowledgments

Any book is a product of many peoples' efforts, but you will benefit from knowing two very resourceful people who were especially important characters in bringing the ideas of this book to light.

One is Yukio Kitsukawa, a young writer in Tokyo who painstakingly edited transcribed tapes of Yamate's talks to several forward-thinking business people in Japan in a series of books entitled *Sogyo Yumejuku* ("Next Century Businesses — One Night's Lodging and a Meal"). He condensed all of this fantastic material into one volume, and got it published by Tama Publishing Company in Tokyo. Kitsukawa's work provided us the inspiration to present our own "remix" of the insights and visions of Yamate — one of the most remarkable but reclusive social commentators of our time — and was a source of much of the information included here.

Editing this book was as much fun as many other games we've played, but it was especially memorable thanks to the participation of Carolie Coffey. She acted as the "ordinary reader who never heard of Yamate nor any of his ideas, theories and visions," and played the role with her usual qualities of rapt attention, incisive intuition, psychic sensitivity, and cosmic resonance.

In daily life a member of the faculty of the university of California at Santa Cruz, Carolie brought to the performance an energy that at times was brilliant, often hilarious, and at all times full of indestructible enthusiasm, spontaneity and encouragement. Already "new being" enough to know that taking oneself seriously is ridiculous and often sad, she had no trouble admitting at times to not having a clue what we were talking about.

She is, however, a Santa Cruz woman with the spirit of this unique "energy spot" — a feminist, mother, editor and sociology instructor who loves to read, to think, to work with words and to talk, so she gladly consented to read the manuscript. She was skeptical from the beginning and confessed often to not quite believing Yamate fully. Chapter by chapter we met, each time over Yuriko's grain and vegetable, no-heated-oil dinners, which changed Carolie's perception of "vegetarian cuisine" so much that she wanted to collect the recipes into a new cookbook. As we went along she began to speak of being changed also as a result of contact with the Consciousness coming through Yamate. Now I believe she could be a spokesperson on the subject. We all learned to communicate in a new way, to produce a book for example that doesn't depend on words, logic, analyses, scholarship, or scientific proof to deliver its message, a book in which we the readers are not being preached to or taught, but are rather essentially talking to ourselves.

January 4, 1991, we were in Japan. The New Year's festival was still going on, and we were invited to a New Year's party at the house of a man we had been introduced to by our artist friend, Oda Mayumi.

When we arrived we found a humble old house in a neighborhood of rather affluent homes near Ikebukuro, one of Tokyo's hubs. The tiny 3′ x 4′ entrance was crammed with shoes. It led right into a very small 4′ x 8′ kitchen and through this into two small rooms which ordinarily served as living room and bedroom probably. That night these two adjoining rooms were opened up into one "large" room for this gathering of about 40 people, all sitting on the floor around several small low tables, Japanese-style. At the far end of the room was a diminutive, very unimposing man who was the reason why all these people were there.

I had been reluctant to go. My partner Yuriko had actually been the one who wanted to because she was a healer and had been told that this man, Kunihiro Yamate, was the only person in the world who would really know how to deal with the power she found herself exercising.

The morning we were leaving Santa Cruz, we got up early and decided to go for a walk for some exercise, since we'd be sitting eleven hours on the plane. As we walked up the street to a high place overlooking Soquel valley, we saw the most glorious rainbow we had ever seen in our lives. It was not an ordinary rainbow. Most of the ones we see are narrow bands of color, and usually look rather short though they stretch over quite an area. This one, however, appeared very close, very wide, and very long, arching on and on and on. The colors were extremely rich and whereas we had rarely seen one last too long, this rainbow was still there when we returned from our one hour walk. We don't know how long it lasted after that. There it was, off to the west, in the direction of Japan.

We were sure it was some sort of a sign because Yuriko had already been saying she felt that for some reason this coming year was going to be very different, that something very important was going to happen to us.

After Christmas, Yuriko made a phone call to Yamate-san and asked to meet him. At first his wife got on the phone and said we would have to call back at 2:00 in the morning, that he was in meditation and couldn't be disturbed. It seemed his days and nights were reversed. We got up at 2:00 to call and he was very gracious. He didn't have people come to see him privately but we should come to a group session he conducts on Saturday nights. However, the next Saturday night they were going to have a New Year's party instead and wouldn't we please come.

So, there we were squeezing ourselves in around the small tables, kneeling on the floor. The people were mostly in their thirties but there were many older people too. They were of all different professions and walks of life. To my surprise I was sitting next to a young doctor, Masaaki Hori, who spoke quite good English. I explained to him how we had come to be invited and how we were expecting to meet Yamate-san to get information for Yuriko about her healing power. We discussed the state of health and healing in California, how many people had become dependent on a medical system based on taking drugs and having operations, how many people couldn't afford insurance or doctor/hospital fees on their own, how many were turning to alternative healing methods and to taking care of their own health by diet, fasting, exercise and meditation.

He then explained to me how Yamate-san thought and what this group was doing under his guidance. He explained that Yamate-san did no healing and had nothing to do with either Oriental or Western medicine, but, rather, that everything revolved around recovering Consciousness. I heard the word "Consciousness" all evening. I didn't quite know how it worked. I presumed that it must have something to do with higher consciousness, but Hori-san said it was not about psychic powers, channelling or anything like that.

It was all very exciting, however, and something inside of me began to happen very quickly. I remember being overcome with a very strange and powerful feeling that it was going to be my mission to bring this man's ideas back to the United States. I didn't talk to Yamate-san except to say hello, but something clicked.

When we left the party and walked back to the train station we were surprised to find that both of us had the same sensation, the same conviction, the same sudden inspiration almost, the same feeling that "This is it!" Something told us that we should make this our work. We didn't know what it was, or how we were to proceed, but we decided then and there that we would pursue this to wherever it was leading us.

Yamate-san does not operate a clinic, does not see patients. That had been our image of him, but it was all wrong. He conducts a weekly session lasting four hours on Saturday evenings in a rented room. He refuses to be called a teacher since he says we teach ourselves. He acts as a guide, though, since he has a long experience and knows certain pitfalls to avoid. So we began to attend his sessions.

I presumed that since the focus was not on healing, I was going to something like a Yoga class or Zen training and that all I needed to do was like a journalist take notes and in a few weeks would be able to write up a story about this man, his philosophy and system of Consciousness training. I figured it involved, as usual, a way to sit, certain dietary rules, esoteric exercises and the like. I was surprised to find most of the people lying down, some sleeping. Yamate-san told me not to take notes nor try to think, that communication would be by telepathy, that we should have no goals or purposes like healing or self-improvement or even enlightenment, that instead of trying hard we should take it easy, that whatever we tried to do on our own would be counterproductive, that the only thing we were to do was open our whole being and entrust ourselves completely to the Universe and then wait patiently, like a baby in a crib. Wow! That was different, to say the least.

We have been pursuing this lead with Yamate-san. We attend sessions when we are in Japan and listen to tape recordings of his "meaningless" sessions when we are back in Santa Cruz. Yamate-san often warns that we will never recover our Full Consciousness by reading, listening to or studying human words — his or anyone else's — nor by following steps, programs, exercises, asceticism or rituals. It comes to some people even unasked for. Most of us, however, seem to follow the normal path of hearing or reading about new ideas and new insights. Occasionally a Christ, a Copernicus, a Newton, an Einstein, or a Teilhard de Chardin, some person of tremendous vision, comes along with a fresh analysis or startling new vision that changes the course of life completely. This book is not the presentation of a new system, new steps, a new program, or a new religion. It is only to bring to your attention the awareness and vision that this man named Yamate has, and to dispose you to consider paying attention to his startling visions of how life is evolving into the twenty-first century. What he has discovered is radically simple.

When we first went to Yamate's house, we didn't have any explanations yet, nor acquaintance with his "doctrine." We simply went. And through that contact, since it was open and trusting, carefree and unplanned — i.e., purposeless — it clicked. It can be so for you too. Go with us as we visit him again. Go without any preconceptions about what you will encounter. Leave your "learning" at the door. The less you think you know of metaphysics, philosophy, religion and mysticism, the better off you'll be.

A **W**ORD ON T**H**O**U**GHT

Why did you pick up this book? The fact that you have is significant for some reason. What would you like to find out from reading it?

Since this book is written in words it is fair enough for you to presume that you are going to think. If you are concerned about the present in your country and worried about what lies ahead, (or if you are simply going a different direction and find no support for it from the traditional society around you), you could ordinarily expect profound, scientifically proven analayses and insights into your current situation, as well as solid, creative suggestions as to what you can do to improve things for the future.

However, I am not going to invite you to think. On the contrary, I am inviting you to not think and to bypass the usual reading/thinking mode. I invite you not to put so much stock in analyses and suggestions that are a product of thinking. I invite you to read along without getting hung up on the words and logic, allowing yourself rather to open your whole being and let the words and ideas flow through you in a carefree, trusting manner.

I am suggesting that the way to understand life, to get information, to solve problems (or rather dis-solve them), or to improve ourselves or the world is not in thinking — in reasoning, logic, imagination, study and human research. The "way" is in accessing our fuller Consciousness. What I mean by this will become clear as you make your way through this book. Your deeper self will pick up on ideas here and there as I guide you along the way. You needn't try to perfectly understand each word, sentence, paragraph or chapter with your head. Just relax and let go. Don't read this "to see what Yamate says," or to learn about consciousness, or to find out what's in the future. Don't look for the point of this book. It will differ for each one. Open and entrust yourself to something greater than your mind and thinking ability. You will find things making sense even though you cannot hope to express in words what you experience, any more than I can adequately express in that medium what I am going to communicate to you.

Words needn't signal only intellectual concepts. We know they can convey other meanings above and beyond that. A poem, for example, is a collection of words, and yet we know that if we savor the verses in their entirety we experience much, much more than if we concentrate on the literal meaning of the words themselves, individually.

Take this book also as something to be savored and touched as a whole — like a poem — and as even more. It will put you in contact. If you can turn off all the noise of thinking and anxiety to have a message, a system or a formula, you will begin to receive the messages of telepathy, intuition and inspiration from what now will probably seem like outside of you, from another dimension of your self.

—Robert Engler

By the beginning of the twenty-first century we're going to see, very clearly, a complete breakdown of the economic structure of modern Western civilization, and of every other area of human life built on similar concepts of individualism, possession, ethno-centrism and humanism.

If you look carefully at human-kind and the world today (and don't just see what you want to see), you'll notice distinct signs that we are now nearing the end of the current stage of evolution — that stage marked by the thinking-human and the products and extensions of our thoughts as a species.

It is obvious that something strange is going on in our world. Everything on this planet appears to be in some sort of mix-up and confusion, from climate to corporations, from families to foreigners, from people to principles, from the sexes to society. Disasters, recession, violence and hate, ripoffs and cheating. We're losing our trust in almost all the institutions and arrangements that heretofore have made us confident and secure.

What is going on? What is going to happen to us? What of the future? What will the twenty-first century be like?

None of the so-called professionals — scientists, scholars and writers — who are studying and commenting on the modern world and the fate of humankind, see the present as an end of the current evolutionary stage. They describe the future in terms of an extension of thinking-human life as we know it today — more of the same, continuing on but developed further by marvelous breakthroughs in science and technology.

They contrast vividly with the religious prophets and doomsayers who predict the final end of all in some sort of apocalyptic destruction. To the professionals, planet earth is going through a period of great change. The difficulties we are experiencing are simply growing pains, natural accompaniments of any transition. Eventually we will overcome all our problems and everything will be wonderful.

These professionals may be sincere and truly

believe it will happen. They may not be just cheerleading to root a tired and losing team to hang on. The future they predict, however, totally misses the target — if by target you mean the state of things toward which life is truly aimed. We all like to think of our present civilization as very advanced and destined to go on indefinitely, improving constantly. The Inca and Maya civilizations were also highly advanced and yet broke down in a very short time — almost overnight. There is every possibility that our present-day civilization will do the same. Numerous past civilizations were highly developed, then suddenly collapsed at the peak of their power and prosperity. So what is to say that present-day Western civilization is going to be an exception? This is not to be a doomsayer, to suggest that our future is dark. As we go on you will see that, on the contrary, our future is bright. The basis for saying so, however, is not the one on which the professional and scientific predictions which abound today are being made.

Even though we grant that they are looking only at the near future, we have to say they are mistaken because the way they are looking at it is mistaken. They are not looking at the whole picture. They have blinders on — the blinders of human science and civilization. No wonder their observations are out of focus and their predictions wide of the mark. I submit that the only true basis for an understanding and prediction of our future is this whole-picture, cosmic view of life in all its connectedness, over the long span of history from the origins of the universe, and a true assessment of where we are and who we are in that picture. First of all, then, we'll consider what appears to be our present reality — where we are in the big picture of cosmic life.

With our current human consciousness we operate under a shared and widely accepted impression that from the beginning of the world until now, life has physically unfolded itself in various stages. At what stage in cosmic evolution are we, the human species, and all other life? Are we at the mere beginning of a lengthy stage of development, somewhere in the middle of it, or at the end of it, about to witness a transition into a totally new dimension of cosmic reality? How do we fit into that evolution? Where are we going?

The evidence is unmistakably clear that we are nearing the end of this stage of cosmic evolution. Many of the basic elements that characterize the current stage, many of the foundation pillars of thinking-human stage civilization, are obviously reaching an end. Some of them can't go on this way. Others have reached the limits of their usefulness and effectiveness.

First of all, for example, there is the all-powerful idea of making money one of the centrally important features of human life. Everything seems to depend on money. We devote all our time and energy to making money. We judge everyone and everything by wealth or lack of it — including ourselves. Yes, the human stage in our evolution — from which came our modern civilization of an industrial and urban development centered around economic principles — is drawing to a close. Monetarism and Keynesianism (which places importance on public investments rather than monetary operation) are in trouble, faltering and unpredictable. The idea of planned economy has failed, which means that money, its most symbolic feature, is coming to the end of its function. This is becoming clearer every day. The system of centering so much of human life around the acquisition and possession of money looks like it has run its course.

The same can be said of the sacred cow of possession. It is the foundation piece of capitalism, and it's considered stupidly naive to even suggest that private possession might not be the absolutely best way to have it in this world. We in capitalist countries cannot even conceive of maintaining any incentive to work and achieve quality without being able to keep for ourselves land, wages, rent and interest we've acquired. If we go back to their origins, money, land, wages, rent and interest are all linked to the concept of possession.

It is strange that humankind thinks of possession as a given. When did we humans begin having the delusion that we first had to possess what we needed or wanted — as though possession were an inherent right? This is a serious problem because in nature there is no such thing as possession, no matter where you look for it. Right at the beginning we have to get that straight. It is only the human species that has done this unnatural thing, made it almost an essential feature of existence — a basic human right. Nowhere else does this exist in nature.

The word "basic" in the phrase "basic human rights" clearly illustrates our belief that such rights as to own money, land, wages, rent and interest are rooted or inherent in each of us. We even speak in terms of possessing our souls and bodies! In none of the constitutions of the modern Western nations, all of which are efforts to work out or delineate the specifics of human rights, is there recognition that our bodies are given by nature, that we don't possess them, that they are simply links in the long chain of earth life in its completely natural state.

Take, for example, the environment. Let us suppose for the sake of argument that we do have a human right to possess and that all of us pursue our human right to a life-style that involves possessing what is necessary to provide comfort in our personal life. What soon happens? We have the wholesale, complete depletion of the environment — given the present population, the likelihood that world population will double in the next 40 years, and the tendency of everyone in it to try to raise their standard of living to that of the West. Soon everything would be destroyed as all of us, down to every last person in the Third World countries, run out to possess for ourselves what we want in order to live a fitting, noble human life. And, there, along with the environment, would go the concept of human rights.

What about those reading this book who are black, hispanic, oriental, foreigner, poor, non-conformist student, musician, writer, playwrite or, for that matter, child? Are your rights as a human clearly honored every day, in every way? We all know it's a delusion and, to some measure, hypocrisy. We in the leading countries of Westernized civilization don't even extend basic human rights to our own peoples, and yet we feel superior to other countries for not extending basic human rights to all their people.

And what about the basic rights of the other living beings who also have to exist here on Earth — the animals, the plants, the trees and grasses, the insects, the stones, mountains, plains and forests, the waters of the rivers, lakes, streams and oceans, the air? What about the living beings inside of these shapes and forms — the organs, tissues, cells, molecules, atoms and particles? Each is alive, and yet how much are we abusing them, subjecting them to deadening chemicals, stresses, and other conditions that are unnatural to them, and hence acting in total disregard of their basic rights! You say that is sentimentalism and they are meant for humans, that we are the be-all and end-all of the whole shebang. Be my guest. Go on living with that conviction. But don't ask, then, why the world is crashing around us. We have no concept of life or what kind of consciousness is in those beings we so easily categorize as below us. We blindly label them inanimate or non-living or some other listing we blindly accept from our modern gods — the scientists.

Human right then is just as much a delusion as is the idea of the importance of wealth and possession. Taken it to its limits, everything built on this delusion is going to break down.

Another delusion is the universal applicability of Western economic principles. The economic principles that have become part of the tradition of the modern West are certainly not in the tradition of Japan. Here is where the structural friction between Japan and America has its origin, although the professionals do not seem to be aware of it. What they call economic friction is actually cultural friction. The laws of economics are totally different in Japan than in the United States. Distribution systems as well as company and business arrangements are also different. To be sure, the Japanese employ terms like "wages," "rent" and "interest," but the similarity to Western terms is only on the surface. The essence of these practices is totally different.

If the peoples of Polynesia or Africa, or the American Indians, ever modernize, their practices will be very different than those of the modern West (even if they are patterned on those of the West). This is bound to happen, and when it does there will be conflict between the peoples of these countries and cultures, and confusion over terms and practices when they are trying to do business.

We could illustrate from other areas of civilization as well, that what were once strong, marvelous, impressive, seemingly logical institutions of modern, thinking-human life are no longer going to work. They are reaching a limit beyond which they will be unable to function or be meaningful.

I predict that by the beginning of the twenty first century, we're going to see, very clearly, a complete breakdown of the economic structure of modern Western civilization (which thinks its ways are the only ways), and of every other area of human life built on similar concepts of individualism, possession, ethnocentrism and humanism.

The time is rapidly approaching when our half-hatched, human, "lord of creation" religions, sciences, economies, therapies, cultures, manners and ideologies will be no longer relevant or able to accomplish any-thing for our survival — let alone our advancement. A profound shift is taking place and we adults of the world are finding it impossible to accept the message in this flow of life.

The breakdown and change that we see around us need not be fearful or depressing. It is telling us something very clearly. Unless we get the message and respond properly to it, however, we're going to find ourselves with nothing working, no matter what we do. Wake up calls are coming not only from the weather, the climate, the people and institutions of our various societies and cultures, but out of the very earth and the heavens. Some force deep within the universe is calling to us.

Our response to today's environmental destruction illustrates our folly thus far. We view it as an economic, political and cultural crisis threatening our human existence. This human-centered approach has the problem backwards — viewing the environment as a problem for humans, whereas, in fact, it is just the opposite: humans are a problem for the environment. This response also indicates that we are totally missing the significance of the event. Instead of it being a crisis or a threat, the breakdown of our environment is an impulse coming from within the earth itself. It is an urge for us humans to lead a life more in accord with nature or some more original state. The changes in the world are telling us how far we have gone astray from the principles of life in its original, natural state, and what an unnatural state we have created for ourselves in the process. In what way it is unnatural will be clarified later. For now it is important to realize these events are wake-up calls and invitations.

There are other tremendous changes going on in the world, and something unique underlying these changes, making them completely different from any we've ever seen before in history. Heretofore, changes were only in the direction of developing the human mind and the creations of the human mind — science, technology, principles, systems of family, nutrition, education and government. For these developments a great deal of serious study and training were necessary. Knowledge only came slowly and painstakingly. Now, there are a number of changes or phenomena not in the direction of developing the human mind or any of the creations of the human mind. We notice a number of trends away from seriousness. By that I mean they are not part of the drama of thinking-human life and traditional values. We notice a number of trends away from slow and painstaking thinking, preparation, study and training. Representative among the trends are "me-ism," the plunge into dream-like states, and an age of encounters, which we will now examine.

It is said that today's children are self-centered, products of "me-ism." Sony's Walkman is a symbol of "me-ism" in the sense that it creates a space for only "me." We are going to see an increase of this "me-ism." More and more people whom those in "serious" society find so disturbing are going to be saying: "What do I care about the nation?" "What do I care about the firm?" "What do I care about religion?" They are going to be moving toward whatever is comfortable for themselves. They will be more and more "me-centered." As new workers they will be like independent part-timers; the office or factory only a dream hotel — one night's lodging and a meal. "Who the hell cares about school? I don't want to go." "Who cares about the family?" "The values of adult human society are all off!" Such is the shocking direction in which a new generation is moving.

In "me-ism" each individual does only what he or she really wants to do. Most people condemn this as sheer selfishness, softness and lack of discipline. Consider, however, that this attitude might be coming from nature, from life. Take an honest look at our ways of living. Many of our rules and traditions have become so top-heavy and out of proportion that even sincere, generally positive and optimistic people are no longer able to stomach them, and wouldn't, were it not for the the parental, religious, and governmental authorities and powers still holding these rules, expectations, and traditions in place. This situation is a clear indication that we are being drawn back to the principle of life in its completely original, natural state.

After all, we humans were originally like all other shapes and forms of life here — simple creatures of the earth. Only when we started to go off in the direction of making ourselves independent and superior to the rest of nature did things get out of balance. What the children of today and tomorrow are doing, I think, is this — returning to that state of being nothing special, of being ordinary creatures living along with, in accord with, everything else on the earth, of being on the same level as pebbles, chips of wood, and insects — no better, no worse. All living by the same life, quickened and sustained by the one same Consciousness. You don't see animals wasting their life for the creations of abstract thinking such as patriotism and principles, a company or a nation. Having no abstract thinking ability to get lost in, each does what it wants to, what life urges it to do, and in that arrangement everything achieves a balance. That is what the "me-ism" movement is all about. Children today are moving in that direction, as, actually, they always did before being brainwashed by adults. In the coming age, they apparently are not to be sidetracked. In some ways they seem like space aliens, they are so different.

We adults, however, are under the illusion that we are the lords of creation, and that our reasoning, logic, research, and systems make us the highest there is. For us adults to accept any change in the situation we have so painstakingly created will now be very difficult. We thought we were very clever. Many of us will not be able to make the adjustment, even if warned that our survival now depends on it. And the fact is that things have come that far — our survival does depend on this awakening. As a result, our survival seems in jeopardy. The time is rapidly approaching when our half-hatched, human, lord of creation religions, sciences, economies, therapies, cultures, manners and ideologies will be no longer relevant or able to accomplish anything for our survival — let alone our advancement. A profound shift is taking place and we adults of the world are finding it impossible to decipher the message in this flow of life.

Besides "me-ism" there are other signs of the life force at work in the world. Open your being to resonate with the universe and you will notice people plunging into another dimension — a world of dreams. What do I mean by that? Well, it would appear that they are endeavoring to escape the stifling limitations of this present-day, human-thought-constructed life.

Does this mean again they are just soft, undisciplined, spoiled people? You might judge them that way. I would say, however, that they are, on the contrary, a clear warning to us that we've begun to take ourselves and our human-thought-constructed life all too seriously. They are pointing the way toward a conscious state that is much less confining, much more real and satisfying than the one we have been reared to accept without question. Sometimes they purposely put themselves in a dream-like state not governed by time and space, cause and effect. Many times it just happens that they have access to a state in which they are undisturbed and can create for themselves an environment where the unorthodox, or even the fantastic is allowed to flow.

The early examples of this impulse were found in the counter-culture drug generation. Drugs take you on an inner trip, which is literally like going into a world of cosmic reality. You can't live on drugs, however, so these people tried to find means outside of drugs to get the same results. Thus, various counter-culture movements sprang up. There was the hippie movement — the hippies sought to live in what seemed like a dream world, so different was it from the planned, rigidly controlled, demanding life in sophisticated human society. There was also a meditation movement among certain people in America trying to get on some sort of easy inner trip. Many people were part of that generation. Those in positions of influence and authority in proper society, however, pulled these people back to the chain gang. How? By criticizing their unwillingness to be involved. "You've got to be concerned about real problems. You can't just be off in the clouds."

Side by side with these movements was the rock music movement. It was a worldwide phenomenon, with Elvis Presley and the Beatles and at the forefront. Drugs were intimately connected with music, and reversely, music was a drug for the soul. Unlike regular drugs, however, music did not harm the physical body of the person, so you could go on and on listening. The only thing was that there were many cases of musicians taking drugs and dying. The wave of rock music spread to Russia, and people went crazy over it in China.

The third example of this plunge into dream states is parody. The most representative examples of it are perhaps the ones you find at the base of rock music and many cartoons today (though in a broader sense, the Industrial Revolution was an earlier example of parody on the deadly serious crafts' guild mentality).

To parody something is to imitate it for purposes of ridicule or satire. Parodying things is a way of entering into an unserious, un-real state, a dream. The spirit of parody today is anti-establishment. It is even anti-ego, denying the expression of itself the moment it is uttered. To be able to limit your own self is a means of escaping from being bound blindly to any sense of values — whether they are your own values or those of society. In other words, it is an escape from seriousness. For this there is no better way than to parody yourself and your surroundings.

What makes rock music, rock? The moment it is expressed it instantaneously parodies the expression itself. If it becomes serious it is no longer rock; it is a totally different thing, only an extension of traditional music, an extension of the so-called artist, right? Rock, however, is anti-artist. This movement is making steady headway now.

What follows parody? Since the self is broken down by parody, music, too, is naturally broken down. So too is the personality and its expressions — customs, manners and life-styles. All are being broken into bits and pieces. Probably punk rock is the culmination of this — a mixed up mess, so to speak. This breaks down the sense of values, and destroys the values themselves.

Parody naturally brings along "crossing over." What has been considered as belonging to strictly different categories, say, in terms of music, now crosses over the boundaries. Then, crossing over brings fusion of parts from all different categories of music. This type of parody/crossover/fusion applies to all other aspects of life as well.

What comes after such a state is, I think, performance. By expanding the space around each one through parody/crossover/fusion, a scene is created. Now the entire space, going beyond individual expression, becomes a new expression — a performance. While performances were always held here and there, the scale is growing larger and larger until now whole cities are pervaded by such an atmosphere. In other words, whole cities and the life expressed in their activities become a network of gigantic performances. This is how it is in a dream. Society is becoming more and more a dream world.

This kind of life is judged very harshly by many adults. Yet it was the unstoppable spread of pop culture that saved us from nuclear annhilation. Neither the efforts nor genius of the politicians and statesmen kept the various nations from spiralling into the intolerable hatred that permits war. It was the pop culture oneness felt among our young people around the world that saved us. They shared a common consciousness that life is to be enjoyed and that human civilization had become too serious.

If you can read between the lines of what is going on now, you will see that more and more people worldwide are entering into lifestyles that are similar in characteristics to people and events in a dream. If you have that kind of perception, you will be able to foresee what is going to be happening from now on, the direction in which we are shifting, what kind of lifestyle we will be living, and even what markets we'll have in the future.

Before we go on to that, however, there is yet another important phenomenon I think we would do well to recognize. It tends to point up the emptiness and smallness of our thinking-human civilizations. The present age is often called an age of encounter. You have literally one era encountering another era and coexisting today. For example some of the Arabs live in a different era than some of the Europeans today; some of the Africans in yet another era, and the American Indians in still another. Yet, you have all these different eras coexisting on the earth. It is like being in a time machine. Ordinarily they could just go on as they have by themselves, but because of the development of transportation and communication, this is no longer possible. These different cultures come into contact — they encounter each other. The same with nations. The same with humankind and wildlife (nature). Some believe that we even have the encounter and coexistence of our planet with UFOs and space aliens. We have definitely entered an era of encounters between an enormous array of phenomena, encounters surpassing time and space, perpendicularly and vertically, lengthwise and breadthwise. It is truly an era of infinite options and borderlessness.

All of these people, cultures and movements I have discussed in this chapter are providing us a very useful service. They are performing an invaluable task of making waves, upsetting the apple cart, and challenging the status quo. It is a role few of us would covet; it brings in its wake anger, criticism and alienation. In the process these provocateurs are evoking vague fears we have that something very basic is wrong with our thinking-human society. Not understanding what is wrong, we feel threatened. When we're threatened we react with displeasure. This is a sign that we are not open; our energy lines to life are blocked and closed.

By living boldly outside of the accepted norms of thinking-human society, these people, cultures and movements provide us with a very clear preview of things to come. If we open our chakras, we will not be upset, for we'll discover that there is really nothing wrong. We will resonate with them and take their message to heart. We will be prepared for what lies ahead.

We must now go on to explore what that change will be, what the future holds for us on the different levels of our consciousness, and how the problems we have been experiencing are going to be resolved.

It is clear then that the whole universe is in a period of great transformation. Some force is affecting us all, from the most infinitesimal particles of matter, to smaller bodies like cells and organs, to small-size bodies like humans, animals and plants, through larger bodies like families, organizations and nations, the planet earth, the solar system and the billions and billions of stars and galaxies that comprise the universe. We are being drawn into some great change, some great awakening, in the everyday life we see around us and in our consciousness. The whole universe is trying to change; the whole universe-body is in the process of correcting its balance and recovering cosmic homeostasis.

We must now go on to explore what that change will be, what the future holds for us on the different levels of our consciousness, and how the problems we have been experiencing are going to be resolved. We won't get any clues from simply looking at present life-styles or analyzing present-day economic, cultural, political and religious phenomena as you would look at a movie film frame by frame in slow motion. The way to proceed is to look backward and forward simultaneously — looking at the big picture and viewing everything as one connected whole. There is one life at work here, the same Consciousness giving rise to every detail of the whole — back in the dream beginnings of our solar system and universe, and in what extends forward beyond our view in the future. In that holistic, holonic method alone lies the secret of understanding the profound shift now taking place.

T H E B I R T H
O F T H E L I V E - N E T

Cells, tissues and organs are connected inside a body by an unbelievable network of blood vessels, nerves, and energy lines, the whole body in a state of balance and centeredness. In the human body we call it homeostasis. On a larger scale the Universe-body is trying to recover cosmic homeostasis.

What lies ahead? Is there any solution to the problems in which we are now engulfed around the world?

There is, but we know from the failure of the New Age dreamers that it is too idealistic to talk about no war, no hunger, no cheating, no hatred. Wishful thinking about love, harmony, sharing, peace and plenty does not bring it about. It's almost as if the Age of Aquarius was shot down like President Kennedy just as a new Camelot was being built. It seems too bad, but we came to realize that, to be honest, there aren't going to be any solutions that will work as long as humans remain what they are. I have to agree on that. Am I therefore just another pessimist, unwilling to go on trying against odds, not strong enough to hold on until we finally arrive at scientific and technological breakthroughs that will put everything straight in our world? On the contrary, I am very positive and everyone else can be too. But the basis on which I make my contention is not my blind faith and trust in science and technology, religion or therapy. This is not about guts and dreams and leadership. I am telling you what I see, and that is that humans are not going to remain what they are. They are going to be changed.

You may protest that this is only words like the fine words of the New Age gurus. My authority, however, is one that should easily convince you who have been brought up in this empirical civilization of ours to trust only the ultimate authority — the facts. The facts are that a new kind of being is already beginning to appear on the earth, especially among the children of the world, but even among young students and workers.

If you will look carefully at humankind and the world today (and not just see what you want to see), you will notice this yourself. More and more children are different. They have a different consciousness. They have different powers. They have a different focus and awareness. They are marching to a different drummer. For them it is not a matter of being unwilling to fit into the thinking-human civilization we live in now. We could straighten that out with strict discipline and firm will power. They, however, cannot fit in, and we adults are becoming less and less capable of making them fit in, no matter what strategy we try. There is a reason for this phenomenon, and I will explain the startling facts later. For now just follow along with the energy that is moving here. Accept for the moment, that life in the next era is going to be different because of these new beings arriving on the scene. What is it going to be like? Into what kind of an era are we moving?

I see that we are moving into what I call a live-net era. When you learn to see, it will be obvious to you too. Taking the place of the failing institutions of our current thinking-human civilization will be live-net people, groups, organizations, systems and activities. I see us moving from an algo-net past, into a live-net future. Why there was such a long algo-net period on earth I will also explain later.

What do I mean by the words "live-net" and "algo-net"?

The word "live-net" is an abbreviated form of living network. When you're living you're not canned. You're not set in plaster. You respond to things in more than one pre-set, pre-programmed way. You're not isolated and unresponsive but connected and responsive. Live-net then suggests something that is characterized by being interconnected — a complex, linked-together system or being. Even more, however, it is characterized by being alive. Not only breathing, but energetic, flexible and free, constantly renewing itself.

The word "algo-net" is an abbreviated form of algorithm and network. Algorithm is a mathematical term: a step-by-step problem-solving procedure, or a rule for solving a certain type of problem. Algo-net then suggests being interconnected also, but in a way characterized by a rule, by plodding, already determined, rigid, heavy and slow interaction (in contrast to the quick, spontaneous, free energy of live-net).

Live-net feelings are true, honest, sincere and authentic feelings. Live-net people are able to stand up and do what they want to do. They don't settle for a mess. They are satisfied only with what is meant to be right and satisfying for them. That does not make them self-centered anarchists. They are conscious of our interconnectedness. They are centered, balanced. We have seen the appearance in Japan of coffee shops where they have live performances of jazz and other music. We call such a place a "live house," not so much to distinguish it from a place where only recorded music is provided, as to highlight the feeling that the atmosphere there is alive. There is interaction with and response to the musicians and the people who are gathered there. It is more lively! These people are live-net people, and this type of coffee shop is a live-net activity.

In contrast, algo-net feelings are what one shows to the outside, though they differ from one's honest, innermost feelings. Algo-net people are beaten down into submission. They don't rock the boat and they try to be satisfied with what they are given. They have little if any sense of connectedness to other people or things; they are even disconnected from their real selves. Their egos are fed by their separation from or superiority to others, or bled by feelings of inferiority. They are uneven, and they neither have nor do anything in balance.

Government bodies, school systems, religions, legal and medical systems, and other organizations of society, business and industry, small and large, even family values and traditions, have become so bound up, so top-heavy with rules and handed down procedures that they can no longer be vital and alive — despite free will and democracy. What is more, they are all getting so wound up in their own egos, their own importance, and their own little worlds, that they are totally isolated and unresponsive to anyone or anything outside of themselves. They are algo-net.

Human reactions to these algo-net social organizations and media are changing rapidly. People are no longer content with what is just available or given to them by the algo-net. We are reawakening to the fact that we are one living being, all connected, spontaneous, fast and free, vibrant and alive — a living network — not millions of separate individual, solid beings, disconnected, bound and controlled in rigid laws and structures, barely holding our own against all the forces of evil that thwart our efforts to progress. At the base of our current degeneration is a forgetfulness of the fact that we are first of all a living network. We are disintegrating because we have lost this awareness, this consciousness. With this mentality, we are only a loose association of individuals bogged down in thinking, reasoning, logic, cause and effect, research and planning — i.e., plodding, step-by-step problem-solving procedures — or to use my term, an algorithm network. If we wake up and recover our memory before it is too late, we will see what lies ahead.

Any and every development in the live-net era will depend on more accurately grasping the true and honest feedback coming from people's bodies and souls. Nothing is going to stand up to the demands of future life unless it satisfies whoever and whatever it is meant to serve. Whether it is a product or a service, a relationship or a system, secular or religious, it is going to have to leave nothing to be desired on the part of the people involved. What do you really, honestly want? That is the key question of the live-net era.

Algo-net society would condemn this as selfishness and total lack of concern for the common good. This kind of live-net demand, however, is coming from a completely different dimension. We want to be alive! Our bodies and souls are living organisms, so they are meant to be completely live. All the bodies of society are living organisms too. They too are meant to be live. Like the compelling, mysterious box within a box within a box, we are all enclosed in one big organism — life. We may think we are totally separate, independent bodies, but we are not. Unless we in our human body, or the company-body, the government-body, or the society-body to which we are intimately connected, recover consciousness that we are all one life, we will no longer survive.

This recovery is the standard by which everything will be judged from now on. This recovery will bring everything in the whole body of the Universe back to the way things ought to be — alive, connected, fully awakened and in perfect balance. Cells, tissues and organs are connected inside our bodies by a miraculous network of blood vessels, nerves and energy lines, the whole body constantly seeking a state of balance and centeredness. In the human body we call it homeostasis. On a larger scale, the Universe-Body is trying to recover cosmic homeostasis. Returning everyone and everything to the status of live-net is the clear sign of this.

FEEDBACK
FROM THE COSMIC
SHOE STORE

Fitting our feet to the shoes. That is what we have been doing so far. Live-net people, systems and organizations, on the other hand, believe you must make shoes to fit your feet.

The recovery of cosmic homeostasis has been taking place on an easy payment plan schedule, so we have not been too aware of it thus far. The breakup of the Soviet Union, however, and the wild changes in Eastern Europe were certainly clear indications that the planet-body is suddenly moving into high gear trying to restore planetary homeostasis. We seem in for a balloon payment!

Many still try to interpret these events as simply the failure of socialism and the victory of capitalism. Something isn't quite right in this approach, however. Can we be so sure that we are not about to see capitalism fall apart as well — and not before too long? We've seen America, for example, get some pretty clear warnings in recent times. Here again we have many trying to explain them away as normal clashes — between social security needs and the demands of economic common sense, or between options of various policies. In the end, however, what it boils down to is whether the people, the machines, the systems and the society are catching live feedback from the other living beings connected to them — plants, animals and people; whether they are sensitive and responsive to this feedback; whether they have any consciousness that they are all connected. In many cases they obviously do not. They've been going their own way, riding roughshod over everybody and everything. This usually results in trouble, and sooner or later somebody starts calling things to account.

We see daily examples of large bodies such as government bodies, religious and legal bodies, not fitting into the live-net model. Even smaller and simpler bodies, however, are coming up deficient here. Take machines and equipment. Why is it that computers and word processors are still difficult for the ordinary person to use? Because neither the people who design and make them nor the people who use them are live.

Until recently, we lived with relatively little. There just weren't many things to choose from. Even if a machine wasn't easy to use, or the shoes or clothing did not fit too well, no one complained. We were taught to be grateful and satisfied. As more and more goods appeared in the marketplace, however, we no longer had to put up with this situation. It is not necessary to maintain an algo-net attitude any longer.

There can be no resisting the call to aliveness. Even the large body we call society will be drawn into this process of revitalization. We're seeing signs of this already here and there. People's responses to a wide variety of matters show they are gradually waking up and coming alive.

We could say the same of services and systems. All of them will begin picking up feedback from all the levels of the living body we inhabit. We'll be waking up and straightening out our act. This is the live-net era.

Take workers in organizations. Once employed by a company, people used to be satisfied to stay there and they didn't make too many demands. Not so today, especially with employees who belong to the new livekind. From the viewpoint of these new employees, it is by no means easy to work in most companies today. To a living person it only makes sense to use one hundred percent of a worker's ability. Few companies are set up that way, however — that is how these new people feel. They leave unless the whole setup of the company meets the demands of their body, mind and soul. Such demands of these new employees seem at first sight arrogant and self-centered to old-type people, when in fact their demands are an affirmation of the enlightened self-interest of vital, alive responsible human beings.

The old-type organizations, systems, employers and employees are algo-net. In contrast to live-net people who are all ears to what life is saying to them from all levels of the living universe, algo-net people are the beaten-down-into-submission types who don't want to rock the boat, who have learned or been taught to be satisfied with what they are given and the way things are. If they aren't happy, probably the most they will do is bitch — at home or over a beer. Algo-net people, systems and organizations then are those that believe you must fit your feet to the shoes. They proceed according to reason, step by step, according to strict laws, rules and traditions.

Live-net people, systems and organizations, on the other hand, believe you must make shoes to fit your feet. They proceed according to intuition, following no particular steps, processes or rules or artificial structures, but rather depending on full awareness and sensitivity to themselves, and their real life situation and surroundings. The definition of live-net is simple then. It is a world of real feelings, true intentions, a world connnected with and growing out of the complete organic life system inside each of the levels of the universe body.

Fitting our feet to the shoes. That is what we have been doing so far with our buildings, machines, commodities and even food. You'll hear the algo-net company employees (and employers!) protesting that they didn't have such an easy time of it as these new people. They endured for years and years, adjusting themselves to the company — the facilities, the workplace, the methods and traditions of the place — before they could do any kind of a job there. How dare these new people make such demands right from the start! This mentality is common to all the old-type workers, managers and executives.

Which view will win out from here on in? That of the new workers, of course. It makes much more sense for them to be able to perform one hundred percent right from the start than to take five to ten years pushing and stretching to get themselves into ill-fitting shoes. In the new era of rapid paradigm shift, no company taking so long to get their people into the swing of things will survive.

The problem, of course, is that the new era people are telling them so, but the old-type workers and executives have no ears to hear. Even their sensible suggestions meet with fierce resistance:

"They don't know what work is!"

"They don't know anything about business or marketing!"

"I've been successful the way I am. I didn't build this company up just to have somebody else do it their way!"

A good example of the rigid hold algo-net thinking still has on companies is the latest, sophisticated machine. It can do fantastic things and is very elaborate. But it is hard to use. Only experts with a lot of technical know-how can operate it. They market and sell it, however, with the usual blitz of sex and showmanship about all this machine will do. The consumer happily buys the machine, but alas, it doesn't fit the consumer's needs.

"I don't know how to use it. It is too difficult to operate."

I'll bet the answer is, "Read the instruction manual carefully," or, "Oh, you'll get used to it."

"But I thought I could do all these things! It's going to take me years of classes and practice before I can perform with it."

Technique-oriented. System-oriented. Right? Not real-life-oriented!

Another example is the company system. We all know about employee orientations — programs designed to help new employees fit into the already given setup and way of doing things in the company. It's another example of fitting the feet to the shoes. Instead of asking the new employees about their feelings, the company gives them a message: "This is the way it is done here. Do what you have to do to adjust yourself to it. If you can't you can split. Maybe after ten years of showing good spirit and proper respect for the company ego, though we may have wasted your talents a bit we may consider some suggestions if you present them humbly."

Even companies that boast of having new ideas seem to be doing the same thing. Their ideas are by no means new.

So, the idea of live-net has surfaced with the new employees. The general public, however, is beginning to fit into this group too because none of the bodies or beings serving them — machines, commodities, services, mass media, politicians, bureaucrats, banks, insurance companies, lawyers, the social system, nor even religion — is live. None of what we associate with human society is tuned to picking up real live feedback.

Until recently feedback was pretty much a formality. "How do you like it?" "Oh, it's nice." It occurred within the framework of the "We've-already-decided-the-way-it's-going-to-be" mentality. There was no use saying what you really felt. Usually it wasn't wise either. Now people are becoming more honest, expressing true feelings without worry about what others think. When an actual user says that the word processor is hard to use, it is honest feedback. The criticism that manuals for word processors, personal computers, and audio and video electronic equipment are very difficult to read is also feedback. So too are the demands of the new workers. Feedback is now very finely polished and substantial. It is not just a formality, and it is multiplying rapidly, even in cases where at first sight it does not appear to be feedback. If instead of resisting or rejecting it we follow up on it very carefully, we will find that it is live feedback that will provide us with clues as to how we will successfully navigate our way back into a live-net society.

We mistakenly thought that because there were no critics of the social systems, cultures and scientific technologies of the past, they were advanced and above reproach. They appeared to do well without going through the feedback cycle. Well, so much for appearances! They are crumbling around the world today. If we simultaneously awaken to the total collapse of the algo-net society that has become so disconnected with the various bodies of life, and pursue live-net feedback from bodies that are fully connected within the whole of living being, a vision of the path ahead will arise within us.

For example, when we talk about live-net in a company, the first thing that comes to mind is marketing and advertising. An enterprise can only exist on the assumption that there are users or consumers. The way to proceed as a live-net company of the new era is to first plug into the live-net of the consumers, instead of first consulting the mangement to find out what product they insist on making and want to make available to (or shove down the throats of) the consumers. In order to correctly pick up the response from consumers, the people in sales, advertising, product development, manufacturing and management will all be trying to develop intuition — a sixth sense for the live — and even an ability to pick up telepathy.

The most that is being done now is to have antenna shops — retail shops that have their feelers out for ideas for new product development. This is not live-net because it doesn't involve an effort to get to the true feelings of the consumers. It usually leaves the company open to developing products that are tempting to the consumer but can't deliver full and perfect satisfaction.

I once conducted an orientation for new employees in a textile plant. I suggested that it was not the place of this company to simply make fabrics — that in fact that should come last. First they should study the total living space in which the users of their fabrics operate because the ideas should spring from that. How many and what kind of clothes do live people really want (not what advertisers and fashion magazines say they should want)? That should be the starting point. This is called option planning. What happens in the present-day algo-net world of fashion, however? Consumers have to simply accept the given styles, and the designers maintain their algo-net professional mind-set that, "This is it! If you as a consumer can't accept that, too bad. "

This is why nothing but antenna shops have been offered so far. The coming changes are going to be so fast and so stunning, however, that unless you go live-net and start picking up real feedback soon, you will be gone overnight.

If, on the other hand, you want to survive and even do well in the new era dawning right now, consciously seek out live feedback from the public. And don't be half-hatched about it. Don't go saying: "That's a nice idea, but...."

Then when you make the change, remain really open, really sensitive and flexible, ready to call even that new idea off as soon as you see it's already past its usefulness. There may have been a real live need for it till now, but the pace of change is going to be so fast that that need may disappear in a flash. If you fall back into algo-net thinking, unwilling to change, wanting to clutch on to what you went to the trouble of developing at least for a while, you are going to fail.

We are going to see the collapse and disappearance of quite a few commodities, services and mass media systems, even though right now it looks like there is a need for them. They aren't in touch with the live flow; they are content to go on in thinking-human consciousness, and so they will not be ready for the profound shift now taking place in the world. It is hard to imagine how fast the pace of change is going to be. We're accustomed to social change taking place over long periods of time. I am warning you, however, about what I see.

Unless you make an adjustment, one thing suddenly stops moving, then a change is forced on you. You are caught unawares. Then the problem spreads to some other part of the operation, and another, and another until you are forced to make changes all the way up the organization (if it is structured that way). Many businesses, organizations, social bodies and systems are going to tumble because they are too preoccupied with themselves to notice the shift.

Whether you are making a machine or devising a system of marketing, it will be wiser to start by trying to catch the live message in the feedback from people. Then put these insights together to make a plan of action. This will be faster and surer than to begin by asking a group of professionals to wrack their brains and make up detailed plans with the help of all their advanced expertise and technology. Start by listening very honestly and sincerely to what the consumers say they want. Then turn your attention deeper. Turn your whole being, your intuition, sensitively toward their real honest feelings. Hunt for their real feelings in both input and output data. Look for options to satisfy them. Find one, then two, and start stringing them together. This is the creative or formation method.

It seems to be difficult for enterprises to accept this point, and so they go on making plans the way they always did, following the routes and methods of the past. They only add new information on to past experiences. Their attitude is still one of looking down from above. You never discover the real or the live that way.

When hunting for it you must get accustomed to observing both what the parties sending the feedback are conscious of as well as what they are not conscious of, what they are saying and what they are not saying — consciously or unconsciously. Real honest feelings are abundant in the marketplace, in the organs of administration and in various social structures. In an algo-net society, however, they are kept in a black box. If you want to make it into a live-net society you have to develop the knack of transforming that black box into a clear box, one into which you can clearly see.

It is true that in some respects people don't know what they want. I think it is a role of live-net industry to help them experience that for once, or clarify it if they were never encouraged to do so. You've got to get the snowball rolling. If you do that, then you get a reaction. This in turn suggests real life feedback options. That in turn provides the opportunity for more real-feelings feedback. Gradually you get a good cycle going, and the smoother you make it the faster the feedback will come.

An example of this snowball method is an experiment that was done on a radio station of Nippon Hoso — a Japanese network. It was so popular that the newspapers picked up the story, and people still talk about it today. The idea was to get listeners to put together their dream person. If you could create the perfect person, what would that person be like? Would that person be male or female? How old would she or he be? What name would you think is perfect? What looks? What voice? What kind of personality? What sort of family background? You can imagine how infinite the possibilities are. It really got people thinking. Even though it was an imaginary exercise, for once people were encouraged to face and express their honest feelings.

Realistically, reestablishing live-net living in its pure form in this present world is not an easy task, since for the time being we coexist with algo-net people, groups and systems that are entrenched everywhere.

It is our nature to be live. One of our primary identifying characteristics is being alive, not dead! Since life on earth has become deadened with top-heavy rules, traditions and activities that have become imbalanced, out of focus, and increasingly fatal, we are experiencing, at all levels of our being, the impulse of life to return to a more balanced, living network form of existence. Therefore I have predicted that the future of life for us on this earth will be characterized by a switch from algo-net to live-net living.

Later in this book you're going to find out why and how we temporarily came to be algo-net. Right now, however, it is important that we consider how to recover the live-net. Realistically, reestablishing live-net living in its pure form in this present world is not an easy task, since for the time being we coexist with algo-net people, groups and systems that are entrenched everywhere. Most of us know how it is to feel the pressure of acting not according to our real honest feelings but the way we should, or the way we are expected to act if we don't want a parent, a teacher, a boss, a friend or society to think badly of us. So we try to shift things at least somewhat so that we can bring even a little bit out of the black box into the transparency of open life.

Both are necessary: techniques for introducing live-net activities, encouraging them and keeping them alive without watering them down; and in parallel with this, putting the brakes on algo-net thinking, or at least figuring out ways to switch it part-by-part to live-net in such a way as not to cause confusion or resistance in the algo-net. Probably, it will be difficult or impossible for the live-net part to grow unless we make this parallel effort.

Let's consider the ramifications of this problem of transition from algo-net to live-net living using business as an example, all the while keeping in mind that the principles can easily be applied to families, schools, handling children and young people, government, organizations and other areas of life as well.

Right off the bat we should note that this effort to make a transition into a purely live-net world will be creating a vast new market in itself, because manipulation of the algo-net is already a striking new demand. So, I can see three new industries growing out of this situation: erasing industries, switching industries, and new-formation industries.

First of all there will be a place for industries to get rid of or erase old industries. Decision-making bodies, real estate planning and other such activities which contribute to raising the value of land in an old algo-net area, or to a change of land uses, which in turn lead to the relocation or elimination of algo-net spaces, will pave the way for new live-net activities. This is the role of erasing industries.

There is need for an erasing function within companies — to do away with old algo-net customs and thinking. There is also need for businesses that get rid of unwanted products. Neither cigarettes nor alcohol will continue into the twenty-first century. There will be no room for products that age the cells of the human body. I'm sure we will come up with totally different pleasure products, but along with that we'll have to be working to remove those that aren't good for life. An example of this kind of erasing industry has already sprung up in Japan. It makes a product called Pipo, based on the English word pipe. Pipos are boxes of candy sticks with a plastic mouthpiece such as is found on smokers' pipes or certain cigarettes, meant to provide the smoker with a safe substitute for the familiar elements of smoking.

What follows the need for erasing industries is the need for switching industries. As the word suggests, their function is to come up with ideas and ways to switch from old ways into new ways. For example, in the old algo-net companies of Japan the type and arrangement of desks and chairs was designed to symbolize lines of authority or job function, no matter how inefficient it might be. When some wanted to change this to be more efficiency-oriented, someone would be assigned to propose an idea. About all they could come up with were ideas such as changing the chairs or the arrangement of the desks. That, however, was efficiency in form only. To be live-net you need a completely new outlook — something conscious of and satisfying the needs of all the living forms that make up the office — people, furniture, equipment and the rooms themselves. They are all living. This is where a switching consultant could help out. In fact, the office equipment industry might include in itself an erasing department and a switching department. Or you could make up a live-net business to totally change interiors so they no longer look like office or work spaces. Make them look like leisure spaces or living spaces. Change or even eliminate the desks and chairs, for example. It's not because you sit at a desk that you work. Sometimes you can get more work done in a very different arrangement.

A company in America experimented with the executive meeting. They replaced the big long table and chairs with a large, round bed, and the executives lay down on it just as they would lie down on the grass. If you lie around on your back you can't say anything too square.

You can experiment too. With trees and other materials and techniques available today turn the office into a resort — a communications or an idea resort. Wear the kind of clothes you would to a resort, perhaps a parody type of clothing. The moment you step in, the transformed environment is refreshing and inspiring. You suddenly feel very creative. The usual routines in the company can be changed to be more like performances or games. You can get more work done like this. Who decreed that accomplishment activities (i.e. work) have to be painful and unpleasant? What is so sacred about beginning work at 8:00 and ending at 5:00? Who made 24 hours the framework into which everything must fit?

I've been observing people in companies for years now and I have found that eighty to ninety percent of the energy of each individual in these companies is spent removing tension among themselves, or disposing of the by-products of such tension. Little of their energy goes into the company's work. This applies not only within companies, but in the area of business connnections outside. Most of people's energy is spent on removing tension. You might as well make an intelligent, creative, relaxed resort right from the start. It will work better.

Realistically, however, I doubt if there are many companies (or schools, or families, or government bodies) with the boldness to change their entire structure and operating mode right now. So, for a start, suppose you make an experimental zone in your company. Designate just this department or that section for a change, and if the result is striking, the idea will spread fast. Keep track of all the information on the experiment and with that know-how you can make a new live-net business out of selling "How to Live-ize Your Company."

Live and efficient; I am not talking about system efficiency. Often when you try to increase the efficiency of a system you end up with more ways to bind people — which is inefficient. I have often been asked to help out in cases where they hired someone to improve the efficiency of their system but found that it didn't work. I noticed that the consultant had gone to a lot of trouble creating unnecessary procedures and arrangements that simply made the system all the more ponderous and complicated, thereby decreasing efficiency. Better to forget the structure and let people display their natural ability.

Live-net industries can sell to consumers as well as to companies. But regardless of whom you are selling to, what you do must not be half-hatched, dragging along with you parts of the old algo-net world. What you do must be pure, complete, thorough and live, otherwise the live characteristics will not show up clearly. If there is resistance, start with a limited objective. With good results you can enlarge your objective.

So you can see that in the era ahead there is going to be room for many different kinds of industries. The live-net concept applies to a limitless number of areas. The trend from now on will be for anybody to do any kind of business, often without any training in it or professional qualifications. We are entering an era in which a sharp live-net business sense will be a hot item for sale.

From a live-net point of view there is bound to be a need for erasing, switching and forming activities. It will not matter what kind of organization or work is being done — making machines, serving people, dealing with children, or even brokering stocks and bonds. If you know the process of breakdown you should be able to come up with suggestions for the buildup of new products or services.

When we talk about live-net we are not talking about "live" in the ordinary, common sense of that which is living — which we usually limit to plants, animals and humans. The concept is much broader and deeper, because live-net is based in the eco-system. It presumes a consciousness that everything is live! Have you ever noticed how a room perks up when you give it some attention like cleaning and rearranging; or a garden when you spend some time fixing up the plants, flowers, bushes and trees; or your car, house, or sidewalk? They respond to that. Be careful next time you curse them, ignore them or treat them badly. They are alive in their own way. They have their own form of consciousness and sensitivity — superior to that of us humans.

Everything is interconnected in the intricate labyrinth or living network of existence. This includes desks and chairs, art work, tools, machines, our cars, our rooms, our houses, systems, groups and organizations, rocks, mountains, rivers, streets and buildings, villages, cities, nations, planet Earth, the sun, the stars, the solar system, the universe, and yes, space. So we have to expand and deepen the idea of live to take in that viewpoint — an approach that, unfortunately, has not been taken often enough yet. A live-net industry in a field such as engineering, for example, will one day soon be designing live tools and machines to fit the biological and psychological functions of the human being. We will have a new field — human engineeering. We humans make words, tools and systems that are extensions of ourselves. Most people consider them wonderful and efficient, but few, unfortunately, consider these extensions living and alive. Appreciating the life in them is a matter of switching our mindset, awakening our consciousness. In the near future, however, we may even be producing products that are as obviously alive as the babies we now create.

Starts have been made in this direction, but application of this all-inclusive concept of "live" is, so far, very limited. Inevitably people make a division or distinction between what is live and what is not. This no doubt goes back to the practice of polarized categorization that has been typical of the modern era — everything divided into organic and inorganic, active and inert, animate and inanimate, according to criterion decided on by the experts in various scientific fields. This is, however, a mosaic thinking approach. By that I mean one with the characteristics of a mosaic — simply placing separate, individual, fragmented little pieces side by side, to create the impression of a wholly integrated unity, whereas in reality what you have is not a unity at all and therefore cannot be alive. Unless we rethink this matter, the concept of live will continue to be limited to a very exclusive domain.

For this reason, live-net people will flourish best with a back-up or someone on their side to help cultivate them when they are trying to get started. The difficulties they are encountering lie most with the algo-net systems and organizations rather than with individuals. There are people out there who feel the need for live-net changes. Let's go on and try to get a deeper understanding of the situation out of which live-net feelings and ideas are trying to grow. From that we will look deeper into what can be done to promote and cultivate live-net changes in companies, families and schools, in the marketplace, in government bodies, in communities and society in general.

We need to look at some of the people or groups in the old-type companies who seem impelled to shift into a twenty-first century mode of living.

The pace of the paradigm shift from algo-net to life-net life is increasing. As a result of this we have deeper and more rapidly widening gaps between generations. This situation is one of the major factors accounting for the difficulty experienced in making live-net changes in families, schools, and general society because, naturally, very few of them are formed according to generations. This is one very important situation we have to understand if we are going to make pleasant progress toward the live-net world of tomorrow.

Generation gaps affect families, schools, and other groups in society, but let's look at the phenomenon of generation gaps in the context of business — an area of life that currently affects almost everyone. Since you have numerous analyses of the generation gaps in America, the differences between your "boomers" and "busters," I think it will be interesting and informative to illustrate here with a brief analysis of the generation gaps we have in Japan.

The generations are intermixed in most companies. The generations are intermixed in most markets also, although there should be markets for specific generational segments—say, for example, for young people. There should be a market for teenagers, for early twenties, late twenties, early thirties and late thirties. Since there aren't, however, and since there are wide gaps in the way these markets act, it is difficult to get a live-net snowball rolling, one that allows complete authenticity and spontaneity. No methodology has been devised to make the shift smooth. The same thing is as true for homes, schools and businesses which are visible as for markets and society which are not.

Entrepreneurs today are a little different than their counterparts before them. In the past, entrepreneurs had to apprentice themselves to the industry in which they hoped to work. Only after they learned the ropes of that particular industry were they able to start up the ladder. None were able to survive unless they had been raised in the customs of the industry and were thoroughly familiar with its mechanisms. In Japan today however, things are different for entrepreneurs under fifty. They start out completely ignoring the ways things have been done before, building their businesses on fundamentally different principles. What are these different principles? They differ according to which generation under fifty you are talking about. All of these generational groups, however, are making efforts for a transition to the next era — which in itself sets them apart from traditional Japanese industries. We need to look at some of them — people or groups in the old-type companies who seem impelled to shift into a twenty-first century mode of living. Since they are products of different generations, it will be helpful to grasp the situations out of which they grew. Then we can explore the differing principles guiding them, as well as look at the steps they are utilizing to make the transition.

Those in their forties today are referred to as the "clod" generation, because to older generations, they were "clods" — a derisive appellation they used to express their disgust with these upstarts who were, to the proud and schooled elite of society, as dull as those who tilled the soil. The prime example of this group was the Federation of Self-Governing Students — the notorious Zengakuren," a group of helmeted, white-banded snake-dancing radicals of the seventies.

Companies hatched by entrepreneurs in this age group come and go, appear and disappear. Although what each of the entrepreneurs in this generation bracket does completely differs, we can see characteristics common to all of them. They stake out their own domain, a space which has no social function. They form a network which has no social function. It is an ideal dream space. Their solution to the transition from algo-net to live-net is to create spaces where they can be their real selves or where they can at least make a leap toward being their real selves, where they have sufficient freedom from external pressure to nurture their own deeply felt, live impulses. Before performing social functions, contributing to society or doing good for people, they pour their whole hearts into becoming fully, wholly themselves.

It was the same in the seventies when these "clods" rioted as members of the Students' Federation. It did not occur to them that they were causing inconvenience to others by their rioting. It did not occur to them that they brought confusion on others. They thought they were doing good for everybody by trying to rid society of the stifling, deadening rules of living and working imposed on them by those in power. Their aim was to counter power with power to rid their society of the evil of authoritarian imposition (even though the use of force is itself an obstacle to being live humans). All traditional authority was seen as evil, so crush it — that was the principle of the Federation of Self-Governing Students.

The members of this Federation were and are sick of "algo-ism" and the algo-net of traditional society and its dominating mechanism. Though they are sick of it, however, and though they are anti-culture and anti-structure, they have elements of these within their own organziation. To them, traditional society is changing, but only on the surface. Its ego and personality (its core principles and philosophy) have not, so these former radical students want to overturn it and make up something new. Parts of the old model of society, however, still mesmerize these people of the Students' Federation generation.

We as humans could describe their solution to the problem of how to free ourselves to live according to new-age feelings as a method of creating a liberated district or free zone. To them, the only way to have a space where you can live by principles other than those of the powers of society that bind you — locally, nationally, or even internationally — is to create a space cut off from the mainstream of traditional society. (It reminds one of the median strip on our roads and highways where you can get out of the flow of traffic to make turns.)

Many Japanese are creating such liberated social districts in their industries in hopes of taking that big first step to change. This is the way the shift is taking place in their case. I feel, however, they will stumble if they are not handled correctly. At the same time, I feel that if they simply remain in their liberated disctricts they won't see their way into the new age, because they are too involved in them.

A second form of response to the old traditional society is that of those in their thirties, who are referred to as the "wet blanket generation." As they were growing up they met with enough resistance to their new ideas to feel frustrated, but not enough to make them explode, so they didn't have the incentive to fight. They suppress their differences and try to do things in a calm way. They try to be accepted. They have many of the same feelings the Zengakuren generation had, but not the spirit. Yet they are rebellious. So they use the "wet blanket" approach rather than rebel openly as the radical students of the seventies did. They too could form liberated districts that don't follow the traditional customs in an industry. They could drag new age generations into their domain as consumers and marketers. But they don't. In work, their tendency is to follow the customs of traditional society, but as a wet blanket, showing no enthusiasm whatsoever for it.

Their solution is to act as though they have no personality, as though they are borderless — included in the steel-bound society but not limited to its closed thinking. They are still algo-net but trying to shift the form a little bit. They don't want to be wet blankets —

people who dampen others' enjoyment or enthusiasm. They are trying to simply ignore power, whether it be the power of their government, companies, family or money. Unable to ignore it, however, their depressing demeanor results in the image of a wet blanket. Thus the label.

Those of the wet blanket generation don't think they should work in the way expected by the old-type society — seven days a week, from early morning to late at night, no vacations, no family life, no freedom. Though feeling very strongly that it is stupid to work in the way the older generations worked, still they have no desire to fight. The radicals, being willing to fight, were able to form liberated districts, but their younger brothers and sisters, lacking that desire to fight, can't carve out such free zones for themselves. Instead, they are unwillingly dragged into the old-type society. They have something very new in them, and yet it is the tendency of the people in their thirties to grudgingly and unhappily go along with the way things are.

What about those in their twenties? A book published by JICC entitled *How to Become President Without Being Employed* points out that the people of this generation know very little, if any, of traditional society. As entrepreneurs many of them get stuck and fail. If they come up with distinctive ideas, however, what can often happen is that old-type people look at them and just think: "Oh god, what can you do about people like that! Hopeless! But anyway, since no one else is doing what they are, we might as well let them do it. They'll find out soon enough that life isn't that simple." And then they survive! It is surprising what a high percentage of them and their ideas survive.

Those in their twenties, therefore, with little or no knowledge of traditional society, innocently manage to carve out a space for themselves and their new ideas. Those in their thirties only half know traditional society. Not having been under the thumb of traditional authority long enough to generate exploseve feelings, they only halfway rebel against it. They are therefore in too weak a position to get anywhere. Those in their forties chafed under the super strict framework of life worked out by their postwar elders until they felt they wanted to get out from under it at any cost. They utilized the strength of their anti-culture, anti-establishment feelings to fight and make at least some social reform and carve out for themselves free zones.

MANAGING THE GENERATION GAPS: METADREAMING

This process must be based on one clear principle: adjust to the new generation. In traditional society the principle was just the opposite: the newer generation had to adjust to the wave length of the older generations. It is in the young people now coming on the scene that the renewal impulse of the universe-body is appearing. It only makes sense to put all our effort into letting that come out clearly so that we can survive. That is really metadreaming — transcending the dream of previous generations.

We algo-net humans believe it is important to know about the different generations — what makes each generation tick — to successfuly manage a family, a school, a government body, a company or any other body of society today, regardless of which generation we belong to. This information shows us clearly the direction in which society is evolving.

Yet despite all these analyses and the brilliance of the observations about the generation gaps, we have to admit that thinking and using our heads to understand the situation has not resulted in much concrete success. We have had trouble with our children, students and young workers all through the ages. From time immemorial we have followed the strategy of using discipline, education, socialization and religion to indoctrinate our children with the particular value system that has suited our time, location, circumstances and beliefs. Then all through the ages we have followed the method of using discipline, punishment, authority and even police power to enforce and maintain that value system.

It seemingly never occurred to anyone to question why it should be so difficult and so consistently troublesome. The cause was early-on discovered by some expert or other to be a natural phenomenon — adolescent rebellion, part of the growing-up process, something necessary for everyone to determine a sense of identity and individual personality. We accepted that and repeated it over and over to each succeeding generation, assuaging ourselves with the profound pontifical pronouncements of a stream of thinkers confirming the absurd belief. It should give us a good laugh to realize it now; but we take it too seriously to laugh, or to even consider any other view possible.

The reason we are having trouble with rebellious children, revolting adolescents, violent teen-agers, critical young adult students and workers, is not because they were born under circumstances that differed from those under which we adults were born and raised. For sure it makes a difference in behavior and outlook whether a child was born in war or peace, poverty or wealth, in a strong or dysfunctional family, given attention or abandoned, loved or neglected, abused or overprotected, discriminated against or part of the in-group of social power, praised and recognized for accomplishments or ignored and forever criticized, made to feel that everything done was wrong. Studying and listing up the differences in our circumstances of birth however, is a hopeless task. There is no end to it. Imagine as well, the infinite possibilities as to how individuals respond to the circumstances into which they were born or in which they grew up. While some suffer because of unfortunate circumstances, others excel in spite of being dealt a horrible lot, and still others become misfits despite the seemingly ideal conditions under which they were able to grow up. Even a computer model could not cover all the possible variables.

The reason we are having trouble with our youth

today is because a whole new age is dawning — one that won't be like life as we knew it in the past, one that won't respond to the methods of child-raising we used before. Society and civilization as we've known it so far has been based on thinking, using our heads. We have for centuries considered it our responsiblity to instill in our young this thinking way of life, convinced it was a model that has been gradually improved and fine-tuned over the centuries to the point that we believe it to be almost perfect. We enforced this superior model on them, presuming it was in their best interests, for their good, or to make them happy. Relying on human brainpower, however, will no longer enable people of the future to cut the mustard. We have to admit that stubbornly continuing to place our primary identity on the characteristic of reasoning is causing us many problems today.

What identifies us first and foremost is not that we are thinking beings, but that we are part of a living network. In practice we have wandered away from manners of operating that preserve the live-net, and instead have increasingly created and embraced more and more humanly-thought-up rules, frameworks and traditions which gradually suffocate life — the algo net. Yes, we congratulate ourselves for being champions of life. Many of us protest abortion, suicide and war. We sacrifice and pay huge sums to promote the medical industry. We celebrate birthdays, and mourn deaths.

Many of us have parents, brothers, sisters and in-laws who are models of love, sincerity and hard work, who desire nothing but happiness for everyone; who respect authority, support the schools, go to church, and obey the laws. They are convinced this will bring happiness, and equally convinced that if their children and charges can be educated to these values, they too will have as much happiness as is possible in this vale of tears.

Yet, all of these are elements of the algo-net. Traditions and laws can be deadening as well as enlivening. The question must have occurred to you: Why should it have to be a vale of tears? Layers and layers of algo-net conditioning (religious theories, philosophical suggestions, cultural directions) have gradually clouded our consciousness of the living network of which we are actually an integral part. Each of us comes on the scene with that consciousness intact, but well-meaning (and some not so well-meaning) parents, teachers, religious, cultural and governmental leaders have covered that consciousness over with better ideas that succeeding generations of thinking-human brains have thought up or higher powers have revealed. As we will soon see, there was an explanation for that period of algo-net ascendency. However, we are not so much concerned about the past as the present and the future.

The living network is again exerting itself, bringing everything within it back to full awareness. That is the explanation of our troubles with the young. They have that fuller consciousness in them. Under the strong impulse of life itself they are being led to resist and reject the deeply conditioned doctrines of the algo-net period of existence. A new era is dawning. They are part of it. They would like their parents and other adults to be part of it also. But it isn't part of the algo-net mentality to learn from children or young people. Nevertheless, the first rule of this transition period is going to be to realize that all of life is trying to recover and return to existence as a living network. The second rule follows quickly upon it: we can learn the way back to live-net living from the young.

We brought up our children to be normal, to live according to the norms of our particular adult society. We did not want them to be odd or weird. If they did anything or spoke of anything out of the ordinary, we hushed them. They soon learned to keep their thoughts and visions to themselves, and eventually forgot and lost them.

No longer. They will not be silenced. They will not be forced into the algo-net way of life. That being the case, no multitude of scholarly analyses is going to help us understand how to deal with this age.

Only waking up or rather re-awakening ourselves will reveal how. Enforcing an unbending control on everyone is out of the question today — not because discipline was not effective in the past, but because a very different world is dawning, one in which the rules of consciousness appear to operate in almost direct reverse of what they did before. We will be unable to deal with our young unless we read the transformations of consciousness now going on in our world.

Every structure, shape and form in the universe is making this paradigm shift because it is all one life, all moved by one same consciousness. However, families, schools, companies and governments are living entities and as such are traditional beings with roots, with pasts handed down, so ordinarily it takes more than just one effort to change them. They have to be worked on in stages, metabolized a little at a time perhaps, starting from where it is easiest and where there is most need. A lot of patience is required to make the change from algo-net to live-net. Yet, there is little time, if in fact there is to be a breakdown of modern Western civilization by the beginning of the twenty-first century. The process of return to live-net modes of being will be easier and less stressful if we are aware of this paradigm shift, consciously remembering every time there is a crisis or confrontation that we are all one, that the rebelling child or the critical student or worker is part of us trying to recover full life; that if we crush this live-net life, we are crushing our own self and destroying our own return to the full life of the living network.

It is typical to hear older workers say, "New employees won't work. What can you do to make them move?" On the other hand, new employees find it hard to express in words what they want to have the company do for them so that they can live and work in accord with their true, honest feelings (the impulses of the live-net). They have a live sense, but they have not yet created a live space around them nor have they found words yet to articulate what they are going through. They may not even be aware of it at all. So they can't say clearly what they want. They ask for abstract conditions such as a set-up in which they can work in a live way. They ask for policies that will make it possible for them to begin working right away in accord with their true feelings. They will say to senior workers, "You have experience. Things have been done in a certain way. Can't we try other ways though?" or "Can't you let me have an environment in which I can try some other ways?" Their demands are very vague. Those on the company side, however, still have not come up with any idea of what to provide or in what way to provide it so as to draw out the enterprising new live-net potential of the new workers.

There are considerate individuals in every company who sincerely try to understand the young people. They will sit down and talk things over with them. Yet they do so with a view to winning them over, getting them to understand the existing organization of the company, or guiding them into algo-net ways of thinking and acting. By doing so they are unconsciously killing off parts of the live-net of these young people. In other words, they are imposing their algo-net way of thinking on them.

The algo-net way is to get newcomers to conform, to force them, if necessary, to accept and get used to things in the family, school, company, government or other social unit they are joining. Despite the fact that these considerate people think they are kind, the truth is they are making these young people feel stressed and burdened with the ponderous weight of conformity to outmoded values and ways of doing things. The result is that the young people run away.

The thing to do then is to go back to the beginning and this time look very simply and openly at where these young people are coming from and the reality of our times.

We cannot, however, put the whole blame on traditional society. The fact is that the people of the older generations have been able to carry on this long. For them there was no other way than to inherit and develop what was handed down to them — the family structures, values and traditions, the culture and civilization built up by humankind until then. Today, however, since there is a shift taking place in the very foundations of the world as we know it, old methods no longer work. If we begin to see and accept this — that the old ways no longer work — we'll begin discovering a way to deal with each generation and each level of organization in our family, company, or group. A method will become clear to us. The most effective method would be to hold off enforcing our views, no matter how deeply we hold them, no matter how sacred they seem to us. Then next step is to resonate with our child, our employee, fellow worker or group member. If we can recapture our own initial live-net feelings, and can empathize with their live-net feelings — put ourselves in their shoes — they will know they can trust us and will open up to us. Then we will know very clearly what makes them tick. And I predict they will bring us along with them out of the algo-net into what we have been unable to even consider before. (This is assuming, of course, a model that posits the older generation being algo-net and the younger ones live-net. We all know that this doesn't always follow!)

If we consider any group in society today during this period of shift we will notice that each of the varying generations and levels of organization has its own way of developing, its own way of thinking, its own system of coping. Inside a company, for example, you see the new employees at the very bottom level. That level is live-net for sure, everywhere. After a little while, however, part of their aliveness is ground off of them as they are forced to fit their feet to the shoes, and before long they are turned into system human beings and organization people. The algo-net feelings get stronger as you go up through the ranks.

Strangely, however, the very top is surprisingly

more live-net. For sure, the company may be a heavy, lumbering algo-net company, but it also has a fragile side — it being the nucleus of profit and risk. Nobody knows what will happen to the business tomorrow. The top people who have the authority but also the responsibility for the whole company, can often have the same live-net feeling as those employees in the field sometimes have from being exposed to the sun and rain of the marketplace. These top people may be open, of necessity, to live-net ways of being, as a means of achieving their organizational goals. "Customs and traditions are fine," they say, "but we've got to survive!"

Instead of being so involved in the mundane activities of running the company or the office, they are faced more with the necessity of making adjustments to the realities of life out there in the living market. So their feeling is very live. They are exposed to the whims of fate. Oftentimes people view a business as a mosaic of separate, individual little pieces all put together carefully and artistically to trick the eye into seeing the stunning picture of a connected whole. When a situation develops that cannnot be dealt with by fragmented, mosaic-type thinking patterns, however, these top people can't escape realizing the contrast between algo-net and live-net. When at times they can't see an inch ahead of themselves, it helps them to carry on if they have the feeling they are in an immense living network. This is a very live feeling. (The live-net consciousness of the workers in the marketplace is slightly different because it comes simply from their being out there in touch with live customers.)

Since any grouping is a living being, it is after all alive, no matter how much it is made of traditions, systems and machines. If we have this clearly in mind, we will understand how detrimental it can be to silence, stymie or kill the live-net sense and feelings of the new generation within a traditional algo-net group.

In the coming era of paradigm shift, it is the traditional group that must adjust to the live-net way of being of the new generations. Families, schools, companies, governments and nations too will all have to face up to the fact that the live space of the coming generation is profoundly different. This may not be clearly visible yet, but it will surely be evident before long. When it is, those of us in the old algo-net groupings will have to accept it, develop it and gradually adjust ourselves to it. We should be working on just such a method now. It is not just a problem of how to get through to the children or hold the family system together. It is not just a problem of how to keep young people in school, or stop the violence in our societies. It is not just a problem of how to get people into the company or how to keep them in the company. It involves every aspect of life in the future. We need to be taking concrete measures to deal with the profound shift now occuring in the world.

This process must be based on one clear principle: adjust to the new generation. Wherever there are different generations living, studying, or working together in any group, organization or body, the principle must be for the older generation to discover and make an effort to unite with and champion the true, honest feelings of the younger ones. (In traditional society the principle was just the opposite: the newer generation had to adjust to the wave length of the older generations.) It is in the young people now coming on the scene that the renewal impulse of the universe-body is appearing. It only makes sense to put all our effort into letting that come out clearly so that we can survive. That is really metadreaming — transcending the dream of previous generations.

THE LIMITATIONS OF SCIENCE

ㄹ1

It is becoming increasingly clear that as a result of science, the consciousness of most modern humans has become a very limited, restricted power. Accessing full consciousness is not difficult. The difficulty comes from mental blocks thrown up by systems that oddly enough are supposed to enhance our knowledge and expand our consciousness. Reasoning! Logic! Cause and effect! They are what are slowing us down. Shaking off their hold on our minds, freeing ourselves from their tight grip — this is the difficulty.

The shift to a live-net society is part of and clearly indicative of a paradigm shift underway in the world. In order for us to correspond to it and survive, dramatic alterations seem to be in order and in fact are already taking place. A paradigm is a pattern, a model, ideal, or standard. A paradigm shift in the world then would be a change in the fundamental pattern of life. It suggests that the world, or life, is definitely altering its basic direction from the ideal currently accepted to something profoundly different. A new model perhaps? Maybe a return to a past model we have strayed from? Or maybe a combination? No wonder then, that simply stating there is a paradigm shift going on leaves a void in understanding urgently wanting to be filled. This problem is at the root of our existence.

To understand and resolve the questions that certain indisputable facts and phenomena are raising today, we have to go back to our origins and look directly, simply and carefully at those beginnings. We also have to examine how we human beings, our societies and civilizations have behaved over the centuries since we originated on the scene. If we really want to get down to the bottom of these questions, we have to plunge into the question of whether we are more than human. This we will do in later chapters.

Before we do any of this, however, we have to satisfy ourselves as to the validity of a force that has exercised and continues to hold a tremendous sway over human life and understanding — that of science.

Before science came along, it would seem that as far back as we have any record, we humans relied heavily if not at times exclusively on the great personages of revealed religion and philosophy for our ideas about our origins, the purpose of our existence, and the guidelines for carrying out those goals. These ideas, however, proved less than satisfactory in terms of answering the questions of existence that gnawed at us, especially the questions of how to understand and correct the problems of suffering and evil, and what is going to happen to us in the future as humans on this earth and after death. In recent centuries, another category of guides jumped in with new rules for framing the questions, proclaiming a better way for us to address the reality of our situation. These were the scientists. How have they done? Do they have the answers?

The only world many people today actually know about is the phenomenal, empirical world — that which can be seen with our eyes or with scientific instruments such as microscopes and telescopes. Anything beyond that is unknown to most. The unknown may be accepted though unknown; that is faith. A sizable group of people take this position. Or, because it is unknown, it is totally denied by many other people. The scientists belong to this category, firmly convinced that what seems like spiritual or non material is just material reality that is as yet unexplained. Give them time and they will figure out how it works. Well, what is the truth? Is there a spiritual reality as well as a material reality or not? Or is there perhaps no actual material reality? What is real, what is not?

No matter how much we try we will never arrive at the truth if we only pursue the world of phenomena, the world of cause and effect, time and space. The impotence of science to explain life, to discover viable new ways to organize human life and create a sustainable ecosystem, as well as its apparent inability, even unwillingness, to quest and probe beyond the material world into the realms of spirituality or metaphysics, is a clear example of this. No matter how far we investigate the life of the world scientifically — biologically, then chemically, then physically — the explanation of life evades us. All our scientists can do is take us back to the smallest, most original particle of matter, leaving us with an irritated feeling that we will never be able to reach the essential substance of life. It has been pointed out from ancient times that reductionism and relativity are the inescapable nihilism of the modern human being. If we are trapped in the sciences, we are doomed to phenomenology. As long as scientific methodology, empiricism, is used, we are condemned forever to going around in circles, in time-consuming, complicated efforts to obtain impossible-to-get information.

Scientists insist on remaining completely detached from anything which postulates the existence of non-phenomenal reality. Interestingly enough, however, some of the greatest among them, Newton and Einstein for example, got their great insights from inspiration, intuition or psychic sources. Then, to avoid ridicule, they worked to find proofs for their theories, after which they presented their findings in traditional scientific methodology, bowing to the pressure exerted by their scientific colleagues.

The pressure of this bias of modern science toward the phenomenal has conditioned us and is still very much with us today. Wanting to subject ideas to a careful empirical scrutiny had its usefulness at a time when religious leaders were trying to force on us humans clearly untenable views with regard to physical phenomena. The case of Galileo is classic. His attempts to investigate the nature of reality via his use of the telescope met with great resistance from the scholarly monks and priests. They refused to look through his telescope, fearing that empirical facts would embarrass them, prove them wrong and force them to change their mind-set (getting them in trouble with their superiors). Today, however, we are ready for far more than science can give us in this quest for answers to the questions of our existence.

It is becoming increasingly clear that as a result of science, the consciousness of most modern humans has become a limited, restricted power. Unless a fact can be explained scientifically in a phenomenological sense, it cannot be grasped or accepted.

Take health, for instance. How to be healthy should not be such a mystery to us. Our inseparable link with life most certainly provides us direct access to the knowledge we need to maintain health. There is some power, either in the body or available to it somehow, that enables the body to seek and recover, on its own, its harmony and balance — homeostasis. We have become so captivated by medical science, however, that very few of us know how to listen to our own bodies; very few are willing to do anything to keep healthy or recover healthiness unless the directions or explanations (and now even the work) come from schooled experts in medical science.

(We are also mesmerized by religions, evangelists and meditators who bind us into dualism, and condition us like Pavlov's dogs to make a connection between getting results and faithfully following strict programs of prayer, meditation, sacrifice, and guilt trips.)

The limits of adult consciousness in modern times has also caused us to mystify and view as problematic our other social institutions — economic, political and religious — and also culture and other aspects of social life. We could handle social phenomena and organization in a more life-giving way, as these are all a direct extension of the life of the earth itself. No doubt, however, the enlightened people of our time would ask, "Where does the intuitive consciousness method fit into our modern science and technology?"

Few are prepared to accept rocks, rivers, desks, cups and saucers, rooms, cars, systems, even civilizations as living beings. Most of us prefer to consider them inanimate. We modern humans aren't able to use a fuller consciousness. We have become trained to settle for and use a much more limited consciousness.

Accessing full consciousness is not difficult. The difficulty comes from mental blocks thrown up by systems that oddly enough are supposed to enhance our knowledge and expand our consciousness. We have become conditioned to certain reactions, and made slaves to certain concepts by these systems. Reasoning; logic; cause and effect: They are what are slowing us down. Shaking off their hold on our minds, freeing ourselves from their tight grip — this is the difficulty.

Our thinking has been seriously truncated because of our attachment to phenomenology that is at the basis of Western civilization. We have denied ourselves access to the world that can be known by intuition, by a consciousness not limited to phenomena and empiricism. We were familiar with that world at the time of our birth and, in fact, even before that, when we were in our mother's womb. However, we, the civilized people of the advanced nations in the world, find it extremely difficult to switch our understanding back to its original mode of operation — a mode which gave us direct access to a much broader, more real — even infinite — world. The spell of phenomenology is our biggest obstacle today; liberating ourselves from it, our biggest challenge and opportunity.

The key to freedom lies in the question: "What is the 'human' being?"

I have asked this question of numerous people. Though they all answered they were part of a special category called humans, I felt intuitively that they all shared a common suspicion that they belong to the same world as animals and plants, and yet also have something intangible in them that is different and that makes them different. Many believe it is a soul, from God. There is another more immediate explanation, however.

We are used to looking at ourselves from our own level of existence as humans on earth. We can get comfortable with the attitude that this is all there really is to our reality. We put everything else neatly into categories according to how it relates to us humans as the center of the universe.

A few years ago we saw a documentary in Japan on Nano-space. Nano-space is the tiny tiny world of magnification. Microscopes gave us our first look at a world of infinitesimal size, the world of cells, but now computerized microscopes enable the human eye to decipher objects much smaller still, down to the millionths of a millimeter. It is like going down a funnel in an elevator, down, down, down, seeing objects within objects at each successive level which are tinier and tinier being magnified to a point that we can see them as they see themselves.

From our human level we cannot even decifer or imagine anything smaller than a grain of fine sand. But when, with the help of computer microscopes, we get down inside that grain of sand to further levels of smallness, each particle or whatever it is, is separated from others and moving around in somewhat the same proportion we experience at our level of existence. Infinitely small beings and objects are interacting in little cities, neighborhoods and homes. But to our human eyes all this world seems solid. Even our skin looks solid, though through a microscope we discover there is enough space between cells to "drive a truck through."

Go the other direction — to the world larger than us. Astronauts now tell us that thanks to the opportunity they have had to view earth at a distance from above, their consciousness of the human situation is forever changed. They are newly aware of connections and relationships. The earth, which seems like a gigantic object to us here on the ground level, looks like a tiny speck in the vast world of planetary beings when viewed from outer space. One can no longer view earth and human life with the same kind of consideration.

If we could go ever further out and view the whole universe, what would we think? I have experienced this view. It is like looking at a human body with microscopes and realizing that you can decipher organs, tissues, cells, molecules and atoms inside what looked like one solid body. As doctors have viewed the human body and gradually differentiated the functions of the various components, so I can see and understand what each component of the body we call Earth is doing, what it is for, how it is operating. What I see is that humans are like millions of enzymes or catalyst cells moving around on the body Earth.

In other words, we humans have a role to play, a function to fulfill within the immediate larger body which sustains and energizes us — planet Earth. The function or role we play is that of catalyst. To be a catalyst, however, one has to be in some way outside of the system on which the catalyst is working. If we humans simply evolved from the primates within the evolutionary continuum of nature, something must have come into us from outside of nature! Is it true? Was that our role — to be a catalyst in the earth's evolution? And did something come into us from outside of nature?

A Cosmic Anatomy Class: Ectoplasms and Our Role as Catalysts

What happened was that some life we could call ectoplasm entered into the brain of these new primates from a dimension outside of earth and the evolutionary continuum. The resulting hybrid was the thinking-human — Homo Sapiens — part nature's evolutionary continuum, part thinking ectoplasm from outside of the natural evolutionary continuum.

According to the most widely accepted theories of our present partial consciousness and knowledge, the world has been set up to develop by a process of evolution. To many people it would seem that if this is so, then the stage we have been in since we thinking-humans evolved from primates must have had a purpose or function. Yes, that stage did have a function. Then it can't have been a mistake. How are we to understand what we humans were doing all that time? We seem to have done some wonderful things, but also to have made a mess of things. Was it all wrong, all bad? If it wasn't, why are the religions so hard on the human? Why are we seeing the breakdown of almost everything we've built up rather than a continuing development of it to even greater success? Why do our young people seem to reject the civilization we have achieved?

Understanding why it wasn't a mistake, what we humans were doing all that time, and what the breakdown is all about, will require that we now go a step deeper into the question of what we humans are, (beyond that aspect of our identity which is part of a living network).

Recovering the state of living in that one, big, connected live-net is the wave of the future. The old algo-net, thinking-human separate individual mentality had serious weaknesses and imperfections. It is clear that that stage has gotten off-balance and is in need of corrective measures in order for us to recover the perfect state intended by the Life Force. There is clearly now an impulse coming from the Life Force for us to recover our natural state of full Consciousness and cosmic homeostasis.

Wasn't the direction we took as the human race something natural? Wasn't it part of evolution and therefore also the work of nature? We humans evolved from primates and were the latest, if not the highest, stage in that long process, right? Whatever would provide a basis for saying that we need to get back to nature? Weren't we already nature's product? Wasn't even the thinking ability that led us to separate ourselves from other beings, to possess, to develop science, technology and systems of life in civilization something put in us by nature for the purpose of creating even more developed life here on earth? In what sense then are we to return to nature?

To resolve this question and refine our understanding of who we are, we need to make a few distinctions and look at a perhaps shocking but terribly revealing fact about our origin, how we are related to nature and what our function has been on earth thus far. Time for a cosmic anatomy class. This will give us a clearer picture of who we are and enable us to grasp what is going to be happening to us in the future.

I will put it out briefly here in all its startling clarity, then we can look at it piece by piece to make sure of what we've got.

Let us begin from one given that seems accepted by most people today with our partial, clouded consciousness — the evolving continuum of nature. When our world originated and developed, it arose in a continuum from within itself. First came elementary particles, then atoms, molecules, cells, tissues, organs, bodies, systems and on and on in a continuing flow. (The question bothering everyone — how it originated, and from what or whom — I'll clarify later. At this point, I ask you to simply resonate and let go; let this stream of consciousness flow on. At this point just observe it without judging. I promise you we will face and answer the ultimate questions before we end.) Suffice it to say now that as far as we know with the limited, partial consciousness and knowledge we live with at present, a living, conscious force in space was doing it all; this living force decided on the specific method of evolution to have our solar system develop.

In accord with that continuum, when the stage of primates had been achieved, a new-stage-being evolved out of them. The body and brain of this new being developed and it began walking upright. If that's all there were to that new being, there would have been new developments on earth but the changes would only have been slight, and these new beings would have been fully a part of nature, living harmoniously in accord with the rest of nature, as beings at every previous stage had done.

What happened, however, at that point, was that some life we could call ectoplasm entered into the brain of these new beings from a dimension outside of earth and the evolutionary continuum. The resulting hybrid was the thinking-human — Homo Sapiens — part nature's evolutionary continuum, part thinking ectoplasm from outside of the natural evolutionary continuum. The role or function of these new ectoplasm-guided humans was to be catalysts in an ongoing process of planetary change.

Catalysts promote reaction — in this case, the buildup, then the breakdown, and then the recomposition of life on earth. There was a purpose in this. By making adjustments in the planetary body, our space-body was devising the recovery of its own cosmic homeostasis. Why? Because the living force's developments began to get too complicated and slightly out of balance. The imbalance increased, especially during the stage of the thinking-human, to the point that this force needed and wanted to correct its own consciousness.

Think of a person building a tall tower out of blocks and finding it beginning to lean slightly because a few blocks at the bottom are a bit out of place. As the tower gets higher, the builder must begin looking up, then down, then up again, placing the blocks carefully in order to compensate for the imbalance lest the tower topple over. Play has turned into work! The block builder may even cautiously try to recenter the bottom blocks that were out of position.

If the Consciousness making up the earth had wanted to avoid effort, it could have stopped and cut off the flow of evolution at the very point where things got out of perfect balance. However, in an ultra-science-fiction move, it chose to arrange for catalysts to do the work of making some corrective moves so that the evolutionary flow could continue on. It even arranged to introduce some catalyst agents from outside the evolutionary continuum of Nature. These catalysts were to promote or accelerate changes and developments in the flow so as to restore balance and symmetrical flow. These catalysts were not part of the continuum. They contributed to saving the balanced evolution of the continuum by causing change in the forces of the continuum. Their function was to alter and reconstruct, decompose and recompose.

That is a perfect description of us humans. In fact, it is one definition of the human — as a catalyst, a being, part of whom came from outside natures's tree of evolution, whose function it was and is to change the evolutionary continuum of the cosmos from its previous position. No one else has ever formally given such a definition of the human, but I submit that without an idea like this one, of the human as a cosmic catalyst, we can make no sense of the activities of humanity in society. What is more, we find all our sciences are limited, as they are based upon erroneous assumptions about the nature of reality.

Since the evolutionary flow of the universe is tentatively a phenomenon, let us describe the function of the human, the cosmic catalyst, as one of decomposing and recomposing, breaking down and reconstructing the world of phenomena — the branches and leaves stretching out into the universe. There are actually different catalysts for different levels, such as those which are concerned with the breakdown and reconstruction of matter on a molecular and cellular level — for example, enzymes and nucleic acids. We can think of other forms serving as catalysts on the line extended out among solid bodies, such as bacteria and viruses, and of course human beings which do the same work. Then next there is the breakdown and reconstruction of the totality of phenomenal existence including human persons. This work of breakdown and reconstruction is done by the ego or the self.

When we look inside the self, we find three levels all based on the body which is composed intuitively: the system of skills (hands); the system of intelligence (to control the skills); the system of personality (to control the intelligence). We can define this as the self.

What oozes out of skill, intelligence, and personality (the way enzymes and nucleic acids ooze out of cells) are tools and words. Tools and words are the forms skill, intelligence and personality take as they emanate out into the world. When skill, intelligence and personality completely express themselves in the world we call them science, technology and systems — i.e. civilization.

skill ⟶	tools	⟶ technology
intelligence ⟶	words	⟶ science
personality ⟶		⟶ systems
SELF		CIVILIZATION

It is through the media of words and tools that our skills, intelligence and personality (SELF) flow out and express or embody themselves in science, technology, and systems (CIVILIZATION). When we talk about media today we usually think of newspapers, radio and TV — mass communications. In a broad sense, machines and computers are media too. So also are words and tools.

When civilization flows back into our body, these turn back into skill, intelligence and personality. This is feedback or recycling. Open and resonate and you will be able to understand the meaning of our existence on earth, our function as catalysts on earth.

We must then regard the human — body and spirit — not as just another species of the earth's wildlife, one of the primates, but as a nature form with another element added on — namely that of ectoplasm. The essence of being human, making us so different, is this cosmic catalyst element, ectoplasm. Like genies, the ectoplasms go in and out of our bodies in the form of self and civilization. We are like billions of circulating cosmic enzymes — like grains of yeast spread out through a batch of dough.

To understand the cosmic role of the human then we must distinguish between two domains:

1. Natural evolutionary continuum — the basic domain of mainstream life evolution. In this domain, growth and change arise from within. In this domain, one level leads to another: root particle to elementary particle to atom to cell organism. This is the level of autonomous life, in which inanimate objects and ecosystems belong to nature's continuum.

2. Ectoplasm — that domain in which life is manipulated from outside. It is superimposed over the top of the other domain.

The nature continuum arises on its own; what is superimposed over the top of it are self and civilization. Since we humans (forms of nature characterized by ectoplasmic thinking) have been catalysts, we have been essentially outside of nature's evolutionary continuum.

Intuitive awareness and empirical evidence suggest that our work is coming to an end; the function of catalyst — breaking down certain elements in this stage of life enough to prepare for the next stage of life in this universe — is nearing completion. This is the basis for my contention that we are in for a big change — a paradigm shift. We'll no longer be catalysts. The loaf is fully baked. The life force is changing the course.

That is a summary explanation of the human situation. You'll see what I mean by all this little by little as we go along. In the next chapters we'll be looking at evidence for this ectoplasm, evidence of our role as catalysts, and evidence supporting my contention that our role as catalysts is ending. For now, remember to just go along with the flow of the words. Don't follow with a critical mind-set, pushing for proofs you can organize in an outline. Don't get hung up in thinking, as pleasant as that may be for you. Open your whole being and let go. Just watch. You will find yourself understanding without knowing how. Straining and using your head, relying on your thinking ability, will block higher powers of intution and telepathy that can give you an experience of the truth far more effortlessly and surely.

AIRPLANES, PARACHUTES AND GENIES: MYTHS AND OTHER EVIDENCE FOR ECTOPLASM

What many speak of as souls put directly into physical bodies by God were rather beings from another dimension which God, the all-enveloping, all-sustaining, life-arranging universe-body/Consciousness, sent to earth to take up abode in highly-developed primates.

Is there any way to settle ourselves a bit about the shocking idea of ectoplasms living inside us and being the explanation for our role as partially conscious, thinking catalysts — in other words, humans?

One way is to look into the myths

of the world. I think it is safe to say that most people's impressions of myths are that they are stories made up in the imagination of primitive and uncivilized people, with no foundation in reality. Lately it has been found that this is not the case. Comparative mythology has developed greatly, and recent study shows that myths are being created every day, even in our modern age.

Not too long ago, scholars of cultural anthropology inquired into the process of how myths were created by certain tribes living in the South Pacific after the Second World War. These natives told stories of awesome objects appearing in the sky and then beings dropping down to earth out of these mysterious objects. Did they just make up such stories out of fertile imaginations? Or had they actually seen something they didn't understand and didn't know how to describe? The scholars were naturally shocked when they listened to the particular stories these peoples were telling. They soon realized that, rather than being a product of primitive imagination, these peoples' myths were true stories of what they had actually experienced, seen, heard and felt — airplanes and parachute troops of modern Allied forces. Though they didn't understand what they saw, they were telling about events that had really happened and things they had really seen, not about imagined beings and events they simply made up as good story-tellers. Their narratives were based on facts. Common to many of the myths around the world is the idea that the first human beings developed after the appearance of some kind of beings from outside of our world.

In Japan there is a festival called the Great Thanksgiving Festival. You'd presume from the title that it is simply part of the harvest celebrations. The main ceremony of this festival, however, is not one of giving thanks for crops, but one called "Receiving a Spirit." It is a re-enactment of the Emperor receiving a spirit (a being like ectoplasm) from outside the planetary system. The focal point of the ceremony is not an altar, but a bed. Even though the Emperor doesn't lie in the bed or even touch it, the bed has an essential role. The bed clearly brings to mind a specific picture which no other prop could do. The festival and the ceremony are meant to be a continual recollection of an ancient event that is obviously very important and one to remember: the ancient emperor lying in the bed, being visited by some being from outside the earth, and receiving or being implanted with this being expressed as the spirit of the sun, Amaterasu.

Westerners, with their dualistic bias of a God who created separate, individual humans by directly putting an individual soul in each physical body, dismissed this myth. After the Pacific War, they even condemned it as the source of Japan's militaristic subjugate-the-world mentality and General MacArthur made Emperor Hirohito renounce his divinity. Both the Japanese militarists and the Westerners were mistaken to think that this myth suggested Hirohito was a God separate from and above other humans. It rather documented a different story: that what many speak of as a soul was rather a being from another dimension coming to earth and taking up abode in a highly developed primate at the instigation and direction of the all-enveloping, infinite Universe-body, which in reality is unembodied Consciousness, the material nothingness being we humans refer to as space.

We could dismiss the Japanese myth as something peculiar to Japan if it were not for the fact that we have this same type of happening remembered in ceremonies in Thailand, Mongolia, and indeed, many other countries of the world. The story behind it all is similar: beings from space (the sun usually) descending to earth.

In Japan there is also a play by Tsubouchi Shoyo entitled "Katsuragi." It is the story about the relationship between Katsuragi, a female spirit, and her son who is human. Katsuragi tells her son that humans were not humans from the start, and that spirits look like ghosts to humans but are really cosmic beings.

Numerous legends and myths around the world give expression to the thought that humans are the result of an intervention from another dimension outside of earth. A legend among the Dogon tribe in Africa, for example, has it that we inherited our unique human life from someone or something that came from outer space. Basic to legends all over the world is that same idea —

that we humans were made by people who came from another world, by visitors from cosmic space. This is one ground we have for substantiating this argument.

Another ground comes from a careful study of the human body. Evidence collected in the field of system embryology now clearly shows that a certain chromosome-like energy substance residing in the brain and part of the reproductive system is a foreign substance — it came from or was implanted from outside. When this or any product of this energy substance drops from the brain or comes in contact with other parts of the body, a severe rejection reaction of some sort occurs. This is conceivably why from the time of the cyclostomata such as lampreys, several earth organisms have had what is called a blood-brain barrier. This is a barrier between the body and the brain monitoring and controlling the flow of substances and impulses between the brain and the rest of the body. No doubt it is to protect the body from this particular energy substance getting past and causing a fierce rejection reaction in the body. Doctors have not yet solved the mystery of this barrier, but the fact that the body experiences a severe rejection reaction when, under certain conditions, there is a meltdown experienced in the brain and a product of this meltdown falls from the brain through the barrier into the body, proves that this chromosomic substance is a foreign substance. It was implanted from outside.

A third ground to support the idea of ectoplasm is the evidence for a presence, in the human body, of a very volatile substance, like a being, that can move freely in and out of the body, that can change shapes — like a genie or squishy energy body. This is clearly the ectoplasm I spoke of earlier. As was suggested by scholars in system embryology, it abides in the brain and around the tailbone. Since evidence for it has so far been provided only by spiritual media, naturally scientists in general do not approve. On the basis of much experience, however, its presence has been known from ancient times, in India, Tibet and certain Islamic traditions. I have seen it myself and experienced its power. I personally know another person who sees such beings regularly. Moreover, recently, photographs of it have been taken with cameras, so there is no longer room for doubt, as bizarre as it may seem to ordinary people. A new science of psychics is growing up to investigate such matters, although it is not as yet recognized by physics, psychology and medicine. Scholars of the new science, however, have taken pictures of ectoplasm during experiments, giving us evidence of its existence, so the presence of ectoplasm is beyond doubt. The traditional sciences are self-restricted from knowing how to interpret the facts.

Roughly speaking, therefore, we have three bases for saying that we humans (selves and/or civilization) are nature bodies into which some element outside of our world was introduced.

That makes it evident why we human beings did what no other organisms on the earth had done — namely, altered and changed the look of the earth. As we examine our behavior, we will clearly see that we (as selves and civilization) were responsible for this change. We have been catalysts, a function given us by space Consciousness through the medium and under the guidance of ectoplasms. We think we have a big problem in our relationships with the environment, but what is much more difficult for us is the problem of the future of our own selves and the expressions of ourselves in civilization. Without clearly grasping this key concept of what the human being is — a cosmic catalyst — the future remains blurred.

It is understandable then, that unless we know what we are, where we fit in and what we are doing here, there is not much sense worrying about or discussing what is going to happen with the economy, or culture, politics, religion or society. It all hinges on the facts of human life. And one fact seems to be that something (ectoplasm) outside of the evolving continuum of nature, outside of the ecosystem of the earth, took up its abode in one highly evolved branch of the primates, resulting in a new species — the human being. Recognition of this fact is gradually spreading throughout the world. Proof of it will be coming in from all directions.

MOSAICS AND THE IDEA OF MINE: EVIDENCE FROM BEHAVIOR THAT WE ARE CATALYSTS

Under the guise of developing ourselves and our civilization (progress), we humans have actually been creating a new environment that will eventually no longer support us humans but rather will be just right for a new being now in the process of coming forth.

The new post-primate, upright-walking species did what other animals had done: hunt and harvest — an activity of give and take with other beings in the ecosystem. Then, ectoplasms from outside of the nature continuum entered these new primates and something strange happened. The new thinking-humans who resulted from this union began going their own way, developing a free zone, something theretofore unseen in the naturally evolving ecosytem of the great maternal life source, nature. This was the beginning. We will see that our behavior provides additional, supportive evidence for the contention that we humans were catalysts.

What we hybrids of natural continuum and ectoplasm did first was to reorganize the ecosystem. We were the original radicals, carving out for ourselves a free district where we could live according to ideas that were not part of earth tradition, where we could live out new desires that sprang up in us, out from under the strict laws of earth rules and traditions.

From our viewpoint as young humans, we considered our ways very natural. They seemed normal to us. However, from the viewpoint of the earth's ecosystem, the continuum, we were radicals, an invading system, our ways unnatural or even anti-natural. We must bear this point in mind. From the viewpoint of life as a community (a living network) we humans definitely represented a mosaic way of thinking and the beginning of mosaic action — the word mosaic suggesting as I pointed out earlier, merely an assembly of separate, unconnected, individual pieces creating the illusion of a unified, connected whole.

The start of independent, mosaic action in turn signaled the appearance of a proprietor on the world stage. There were originally no proprietors in the natural world. What about sparrows, fish, and various animals who have their territories? Their territories are ecospheres, not owned property. (When a lair of lions moves to a new place they don't try to sell their territory to some other group nor have to buy a new territory to move into. They have no concept of possession.) Only when we humans appeared on the stage were proprietors introduced into the play. We began to portion off our lands, or our ecospheres, as assets. We seem to have forgotten this and now take this state of affairs as a given. We believe, as we state in our constitutions, that possession is an inalienable right. It isn't. Possession is not by divine right. This was not in the plan of nature, and yet somehow the idea suddenly showed up. We humans were the ones to espouse it. Consciously or not the idea of "mine" had appeared. From where? From outside the nature continuum, from space, in the beings called ectoplasms.

This possession was the origin of individual consciousness. Our primitive ancestors may have lived as groups and communities, but the moment something got into them to make them want to possess, the idea spread to everything we humans were involved with, down to our own minds and bodies being our own possessions, something inviolable. From primitive times on, we humans were proprietors — in other words, individuals. Whole villages, nations, races, in fact the whole human race, became a mosaic of individuals, each enclosed in itself, cut off from others.

The concept of individual is actually anti-nature. We modern humans, however, have misunderstood this point, thinking instead that being an individual person, with inviolable rights, is actually basic to human nature. But it isn't. It is an algo-net law. It doesn't exist in the natural world. The idea of being individual or completely separate from others is an artificial concept, made up by humans, put in us humans by the ectoplasms.

The epitome of separation from other forms of life is found in the idea of human rights which we humans have formally proclaimed in our modern constitutions. The more advanced of us are even going around the world trying to push this idea onto groups we label as primitive peoples. However, we are now getting a glimpse of where individualism and human rights, taken to their ultimate lengths, lead. Our papers and news programs chronicle an increasing hemorrhage of shootings, stabbings, cheating and corruption, violence, destruction, and environmental breakdown. Still we push on, under the illusion that individual human rights, if really championed and practiced by everyone, everywhere, would bring us peace and happiness. The old algo-net mind-set is still firmly in place.

Nevertheless, there is now an impulse being felt to go back to our beginnings and take a new look at this.

Most of the excitement (I'm using human words of course) of the early acts of the Earth Story was the unique plot of having us humans think in order to know what to do. As instinct faded and intuition dulled, we nature/ectoplasm hybrids had to slowly figure things out. It was painstaking effort, accompanied by mistakes and failures. The seemingly mistaken directions humans took, of course, were not mistaken at all in the overall picture. We humans were moving things very definitely toward an environment Nature was not given the role to achieve.

We gradually evolved from the simple killing ways of animals to more sophisticated methods of seizure, and later discovered that a better way to get what we wanted from the world around us was not to use force but rather to trick the animals and plants and other humans. This was fraud — you obtain something from another after looking as though you were being useful to the other party. For example, we said to the rice plant: We'll increase your species for you. We raised crops but in the end ate them all up. We did the same to cows. We bred and fattened them, all along saying, "How sweet." In the end we ate them. Fraud was at the basis of our present-day agricultural and stock-farming industries.

Among humans, exchange took the form of mutual deceit — the start of which was buying and selling.

Therefore, the basis of trade is fraud, trickery and deceit. To put it another way, those who are not good at fraud do not make good merchants. Profit also had its beginning here. There is no profit without a type of fraud. A totally fair exchange leaves you with a profit of zero. So buying and selling are a form of mutual fraud: acquire something as cheaply as possible and sell it at as high a price as possible. Credit, lending or borrowing, and interest followed. (Remember we are not judging. We're just looking at how our catalyst role developed. It was interesting and effective, as we will see.)

At any rate, what grew out of this idea of each human being existing as an individual and having rights distinct from other beings on the earth was the idea that what you created as an individual belonged to you. With that came other new ideas: the idea of work, and remuneration for work. Tadpoles gathering food to live, bees gathering honey into their hives and plants producing flowers are not working. Work came in with us humans. How was that? We only changed matter and information and added nothing new to the natural world, yet we thought we were creating added value. This we called work and we began to regard it with an abnormal attachment. This led to the feeling of having to work, and to the idea of being entitled to remuneration for our work since what we did as individuals belonged to us.

In turn this reinforced the whole individualist mentality. Each village began to feel individual and separate, proprietor of its own territory, work and production. When a conflict with another village arose, as it naturally would, the conflict could lead to massacres and wars. Even among individual persons competition and conflict arose, sometimes leading humans to kill each other. Struggle and killing our own kind were human characteristics. There was nothing like them among the plants and animals. Certain animals might fight over food or a female or other concrete matter, but only humans fought and killed each other over abstract ideas like ownership and rights.

Anthropologists have never understood the exact cause of this, but have figured that it had to be the result of something in human beings uncommon to nature. Religious leaders, scholars and professionals have been equally at a loss, unaware that the catalyst role of humans is at the very root of the problem. They go in circles, protecting their worn-out theories — as good catalysts were supposed to do. The time seems to have come, however, when we are no longer to do so. There is a new impulse being felt in the world today — to remember back to the beginning and find out what really happened, to have a more satisfying realization of how we humans came on the scene and why. Some distant memory is stirring in the consciousness of all living beings. As the memory returns we are waking up to the fact that what we were doing as catalysts was simply play and make-believe.

Part of the reason may be the fear that if we don't alter our course soon we're going to self-destruct. Recognizing our role as catalysts, however, will enable us to understand and appreciate why I do not see self-destruction as part of our future. In contrast to the insider participation in the continuum that characterized the natural world, we humans evolved outside the continuum, in an interruptive and disconnected way, distinct from the rest of Earth's living ecosystem. As we invaded nature, our role clearly became alteration and re-creation of the ecosystem. Over and over we repeated this same pattern: breakdown and new formation. Although it is sure that we destroyed, nevertheless, in the process of creating something new we tried to adjust to the new environment created so as not to endanger our own existence. We adapted while destroying.

If we were simply one more species of organism in the earth continuum, we would have gone extinct pulling the unnatural tricks we did. Locusts go extinct in the year following a great outburst or plague. It is reasonable to assume that such a mechanism would have been triggered by the great outburst of billions of individual humans breaking down and remaking the natural environment. Why wasn't it? Why haven't we humans gone extinct? Because we have had a role to play in the cosmos — the role of catalyst. The plan came from our infinite space mind. It was to give rise to individuals who act as catalysts to destroy and re-create the earth through their individual selves and their products (civilization). We humans will disappear, but not through a process of self-destruction. We will be phased out through the process of evolution as our catalyst role winds down. That, however, is taking place right now, so those catalysts who want to clutch on to their identity in that role will no doubt feel anxiety.

We humans have been breaking down and re-creating the very environment we artificially created — civilized society. Furthermore, if we look at the way we use chemicals to raise food and the way we choose, prepare and eat our food, the way we create stress for ourselves with unnecessary work, competition and anger, we will realize we are breaking down and re-creating our own bodies (that ecosphere belonging to the nature continuum, that part of us that is autonomous). This is how far we have come.

All phenomena, whether they be organisms or beings belonging to the sphere of physics and chemistry, follow two basic laws. One is the law of commonness, meaning that various materials all circulate among those with whom they are compatible, with whom they have everything in common: cells with cells, molecules with molecules. Atoms can migrate from molecule to molecule. Elementary particles move from atom to atom. So they share the same field of options. Option feedback is a basic principle. The law of common options is the first law of phenomena.

The second law is that of specificity. Although sharing a common basis, each looks at first sight as though it were an individual having its own specific existence, characteristics and function. Mixed options is the second law. Specificity arises from a specific mixture of options.

Every phenomenal being in the universe arises according to these two laws. When commonness and specificity are balanced, phenomena arise as living forms. There are sometimes imbalances, however. In some cases there are more specifics, in other cases more commonness. When there is more commonness, specificity decomposes, is destroyed. For example, cells return to being atoms, then atoms decompose (I suppose because entropy increases when there is an excess of commonness). When entropy increases, atoms go back to elementary particles, break down and finally disappear. They return to space.

What if the reverse happens? What happens to commonness when there is an excess of specificity? If certain cells become specific and gather together endlessly, metabolism ultimately stops. Then the composition has to be decomposed. This problem occurs after cells form multi-cell bodies like ours or those of animals and plants — the ultimate crystallized societies. Multi-cell bodies differentiate into species. By adjusting to various climates and environments, they become over-adaptable and divide into species that are different than those from which they originated. Then although they originally belonged to the same species, they cannot even mate and procreate, to say nothing of sharing the nutrition in their bodies with that of another body through metastasis. This is the state of excess differentiation — the problem the earth's ecosystem faced.

Something to correct this state of excess differentiation then appeared naturally on the earth. Ectoplasms took up abode in primates. It was the function of us resulting human beings to destroy excess differentiation. At first, in a form that seemed a little unnatural, we humans gathered seeds that previously had been spread naturally, and began to raise crops in one place, in a mono-culture fashion. This was the beginning. Next we hybridized the seeds artificially, using the technique of cross-fertilization.

We then did the same with minerals, developing new minerals not found in the natural world — for example, ceramic. There was no ceramic in nature. Ceramic is a hybridization on the mineral level, a conversion of character. We did the same thing with animals and have been performing the function of catalyst ever since. We have been doing it over and over under the illusion that we were doing it for our own benefit and convenience as individual beings. However, being a catalyst was the reason for our existence, no other. Our body is kept alive in accord with nature's principles, by the same principles governing the plants and animals, not the principles of self or civilization. The nature part of us lives by the principles of the ecosystem. The other part of us has lived by other principles, given directions by ectoplasms from outside of the earth's continuum. Our function has been that of meta-catalyst, endlessly breaking down and rebuilding, decomposing and recomposing minerals, plants, animals, and even our own bodies.

Ultimately, when this catalyst function of decomposing and recomposing the earth and the ecosystem developed further, it separated itself, as we saw earlier, from the head and hands of us humans and went out of our body. In one era, language came into play as the means for creating systems written in words. With these systems we were able to begin controlling society. Tools and machines came out of us as extensions of our hands, ushering in the Industrial Revolution. The first Industrial Revolution in the middle of the eighteenth century was a radical change in skills. It was, in a certain sense, an industrial revolution centered around things, and resulted ultimately in technology.

In the next stage, the so-called modern era, the functions of our cerebral nervous system oozed out, materializing outside of us. The stage of industrial revolution centering around the intellect began, resulting in science. Since the functions of the cerebral nervous system are controlled by the personality, when this oozed out, the functions of human personality took on an existence outside, as systems. Even though the industrial revolution of skills is still going on, henceforth the industrial revolutions of the intellect and personality will not only advance in parallel with it but overlap and cover it. They will develop much much more, beyond self and civilization which were catalyst functions. They will radically change the relationship between individual and social functions in the division of labor.

This is, I think, what Alvin Toffler meant by power shift, but though he brought up many facts in his book, he did not clearly determine the reason why things are happening the way they are. This can be understood rather simply, however, if we look at the paradigm I have described.

According to my paradigm of the world, things are happening the way they are because we humans have brilliantly performed our role as catalysts. We are like the bacteria Yatri mentioned in his book *Unknown Man* — certain bacteria which, eons earlier in their pursuit of progress (metabolizing glucose), developed an oxygen-filled atmosphere which eventually led to their demise and instead provided an environment perfect for humans. Now, we humans, under the guise of developing ourselves and our civilization (progress), have actually been creating a new environment that will eventually no longer support us humans but rather will be just right for a new being now in the process of coming forth.

This is the cut-and-dried view of the human — not the emotionally charged vision we have of the fantastic greatness of our race. As phenomena, we are the same as pebbles, chips of wood, insects, cells, molecules and atoms, integral elements of the living network with a role to play. If we look at ourselves in this way, however, everything makes sense. From our behavior we have evidence that we were catalysts.

THE CURTAIN
COMES DOWN:
THE END OF THE
CATALYST ROLE

We think we are developing ourselves to the fullest by marshalling all the rest of the world for the benefit of self and the products of self, i.e. civilization, whereas, in fact, when we do this, we are actually setting the stage for our demise. We have a grave concern for earth life. However, should we insist on trying to protect and further it through the agencies of self and civilization, matters will only worsen.

We are aware that cultures and civilizations are products of the function of the self, but we are for the most part unaware that these products we've made in turn serve the function of cosmic catalysts. As a result of this ignorance, we've lost touch with their meaning at every level. Consequently our difficulty forecasting what will happen to them from now on. After all, however, no activity or system of civilization — whether it be economic, political, religious or cultural — has any meaning other than that of cosmic catalyst: one hundred percent breakdown then rebuilding; completely destroying then re-creating.

Because of not knowing about our catalyst role, we have been and continue to be confused on several points. First of all, we have been way off the track on the point of our identity. We have all along come to identify ourselves as composite sums of certain intelligence, skills and personality traits (self) and the products or expressions of the self — science, technology and systems (civilization). Those elements are qualities attached to us by the ectoplasm in our brain to make us play the role of catalyst. They are like costumes and makeup that enable actors to play certain roles in a drama. They do not make the actors who they really are. To identify with the costume, the makeup and the role, is to be ridiculous. The trouble here is our misunderstanding of the human being. We have made the grave mistake of thinking that the functions of the self and civilization are of our essence, that they are synonymous with and inseparable from ourselves, that they are part of the continuum of life on earth, part of nature. Self and civilization are not of our essence, and they have already been separated from us with their own function.

A catalyst can perform its function only by being separate from the material in which it is causing a reaction. So too our self and civilization can function as catalysts only by being separated from our bodies which are extensions of the earth-life continuum. Human life can work in no other way.

Not having understood our catalyst role also underlies the contradiction that exists in our insisting on the concept of basic human rights. When we talk about our basic human rights we don't think of our body as having the right. It is our self that has it (that is, a being called the self, living in our body, operating under the direction of ectoplasm which came from outside the realm of nature). The Life Force put ectoplasm into nature's upright-walking primates to perform the role of catalyst, with a view to preparing for the next stage of evolution. Under this direction we have always been impelled to develop and display our skill, intelligence and personality one hundred percent and to overcome and get rid of any obstacle to that. This purpose as catalyst has been the driving force behind our insistence on basic human rights.

Therein, however, lies a contradiction of human existence. We think we are developing ourselves to the fullest by marshalling all the rest of the world for the benefit of our skill, intelligence and personality, whereas, in fact, when we do this, we are actually setting the stage for our demise. We will disappear from the stage, but through change, not in an apocalyptic orgy of destruction marking the end of all. How? Why? By altering the environment in which we are living in order to change it to a point suitable for the next stage of evolution. This was not clear before, yet my intuitive sense indicates a profound change has been decided on by the fuller consciousness of our body that envelops us, sustains and directs us — i.e. our full Consciousness.

We now see the time for this change has come. It is right in front of us, staring us in the eye. As long as we continue to go on developing our selves and our civilizations, we are continuing to play the catalyst role. This catalyst role, however, is coming to an end. We are issuing new instructions to phase out this role and prepare us for a new role in a fresh drama about to unfold on the stage of the world. If we blockheadedly refuse to accept the new instructions, if we resist, shouting, "No, I want to continue this play. I like this play. I won't change!" if we put our head in the sand and refuse to look around and see the evidence of a new stage being prepared, we'll have trouble. We will be unsure as to how to go about preserving our human body, the environment and earth's ecosystem — the overall continuum of earth life which we call autonomous nature.

In the idea life had for this particular play, catalysts belong to the world of algo-net. The algo-net world differs from the live-net world in that it is not part of the cosmic life continuum. The algo-net world is the separate domain of catalysts. All its functions are in the hands of catalysts. Its whole reason for existence is simply to produce and facilitate reaction and change. None of our scientific, political, economic, cultural, philosophical or religious leaders have understood their catalyst role. None of us have.

All the principles of culture and civilization which we as humans have thought up belong to the world of disconnection. Take humanism for example. Romain Rolland states typically that humanism is a world of disconnection. He uses the word abyss, saying that we humans (we as individuals) are sincerely truthful, but are separated by an abyss from one another. He offers a very gloomy definition of humanism as a bridge between such individuals. Sartre said the same. His existentialism meant the same thing as humanism. Even if not nihilistic as was Camus' existentialism, it was incorrigibly solitary. It was a world in which one feels violently separated, in a disconnected, mosaic existence.

When we look at algo-net and live-net, the difference between their bases and natures become very clear. On the surface, what is algo-net looks good. In it, individually-based mosaic relationships are adjusted, and problems are dealt with through a process resembling steps in a calculation when we're trying to solve a mathematical problem. In comparison, what is live-net is hard to put our finger on, vague and overlapping, is intermeshed, has no hard and fast boundaries. The reason is that the live world is not a mosaic. It is one whole. Every facet is holographically infiltrated, interacting in mutual harmony, organic and indivisible. Problems and relationships are not dealt with through a step-by-step, logical process but rather by immediate, intuitive grasp and telepathy.

If you had a very difficult mathematical problem to solve, however, which would you consider the stronger: the person who goes to the blackboard and covers the whole thing with complicated formulas at the end of which the answer comes out, or, the person who sees the problem, then shuts his eyes, is silent for a period, then suddenly gives the answer? If the contest were taking place on a stage you would all cheer the latter as a genius of some sort, a wizard!

There is no other way to express this truth than to say that the real live world is not individual-based, isn't a mosaic of individual pieces, but rather is organically and mutually interpenetrated, permeated throughout by one same whole, Life or Consciousness. The algo-net is a world of rules and traditions which are separate from those of the world which has been evolving as a cosmic continuum. The catalysts of the algo-net world are agents of separation and discontinuity. Why would we want to go on having to sweat out an answer over the whole surface of the chalkboard of life in this role, if another role were offered us — a role in which we could come up with the answer without effort. A brilliant mathemetician who enjoys problem-solving of this sort might not want to give up such a familiar and pleasant pursuit; but is it the best way of life for everyone?

If we are looking at things from the viewpoint of our old role as catalysts, we will see only problems everywhere we look — in the realm of health and healing, in education, business ethics and international relations, with our politicians, political systems, administrators, bureaucrats and bureaucracies, our lawyers and justice system, insurance companies, our families and our marriages. If we don't unravel the confusion about who we are and what we're doing here, there will be no calming our anger, anxieties and fears. There will be no solutions forthcoming to our environmental or social problems, to say nothing of economic worries or the future of marketing!

People talk about what is sustainable these days. We have a grave concern for earth life. However, should we insist on trying to protect and further it through the agencies of self and civilization, matters will only worsen. People who push for individual human rights are beings without connection to earth life. We must always bear this in mind. As we wake up and recall that human rights, self and civilization are only catalysts, we'll realize they are only a facet or side of us which has been performing the role of preparing the world for the next stage of evolution. They were meant to do their work and then disappear. We are not to identify ourselves with them or by them. The real us is not a collection of skills, intelligence and personality, or the products of these — science, technology and systems. If we identify with them we will disappear along with them. Ignorance of this point is the reason our existence on earth is now in a state of such doubt and confusion, why we are facing such horrendous difficulties and problems in our private lives and in society.

However, we don't have to be ignorant about our existence any longer, and with clarity about it our doubts and confusion, difficulties and problems can be resolved. This is one major point of clarity: our catalyst role is coming to an end so it will now be possible for us to shed the costumes and makeup of catalysts, the gestures, speech and activities of catalysts, and detach from catalyst artifacts we created (science, technology, and systems such as the family, government, education, health, criminal justice and economy — i. e., civilization). We can let these drop away, and with a nostalgic, sentimental tear of fond farewell to the tragedies and triumphs of our brief hour as humans on the stage of earth life, take a breather, get back to being ourself and in leisure look over the designs of the next play that is being put together this very moment in our mind.

If we want to make the transition effectively and painlessly, it will be necessary for us to grasp one principle that is already guiding the evolving organizational life of the new era: abandonment or total entrustment.

A significant development to keep in mind when trying to read the future is the form human organizations have taken in their evolution. When we humans came on nature's landscape, we were not loners. We did things together. Groups, packs and tribes moved around together in search of food and shelter. We had leaders. Since we were catalysts, however, we gradually began to complicate the manner in which we organized. Observing just the direction human organization has been taking since the Industrial Revolution shows the now-familiar development of distinctive algo-net patterns.

In the ecotype action of the Industrial Revolution, the first associations of people simply served a representative function; they played a representative role. They were forms of union expressed by the term "agency."

When any organization is formed in human society — for example, when ten people get together to do something — the first thing they do is form an association or group. It doesn't have a juridical personality yet. It is just a loose association. The characteristic of an association is that the association does not have proprietorship of its own. Ownership of anything the association uses still belongs to the members who participate in it. The members just get together, each bringing his or her share of ideas, talents, chairs or what-have-you. Since an association has just a tentative existence — simply representing each member's interests, or serving as each member's agent — the law describes it as a representative organization.

Association is always at the base of any organization. Trace back the steps followed in the evolution of a juridical person — the setting-up of a corporation, for example — and you start with an association of promoters. No company can be operated without the relationship of association as its base. Not even a joint stock corporation in the later stage of authorized capital can be operated smoothly without the sense of association. Association is always at the base.

When companies get together to form an association, the association is at first voluntary because it is a link of agents. The individual companies forming the voluntary association each retain their proprietary and discretionary rights. The essence of the voluntary association is simply its representative function. The association only has tentative custody. However, when the voluntary representative association evolves in greater complexity, it becomes a trust organization. The same goes for franchise associations, because a franchise association is a trust organization. The characteristic of a trust organization is that now the members transfer nominal right of ownership. They tentatively entrust the trust with the right of ownership. The term "assets-in-trust" signifies that the assets are now held by the trust, which invests them in the name of the trust and then returns the profits to the trustees. The profits are returned, but while the assets are invested, the nominal right of ownership is in different hands. We can see that subjectivity is gradually shifting towards the organization!

When this process systematically evolves even further, the next stage is administrative organization. In administrative organizations like corporations, the moment an investor becomes a stockholder, his or her right of ownership is completely transferred to the company. This is the significance of capital and corporations. According to the principle governing adminstrative organizations, the stockholder becomes in essence anonymous. Thus the words "...and many others." The same holds for regular retail chains also. Member stores of a chain completely entrust the main office with the operations and powers of management.

These are the stages through which human organizations have developed, each stage corresponding to a different function that has evolved. We can easily appreciate how ownership, labor and struggle took different forms at each stage. For example, as I pointed out above, at one stage ownership was in the hands of the individuals who began to associate in the form of a simple group or association; gradually humans figured out how efficiency could be increased by putting that ownership nominally in the hands of the organization which took the form of a trust; later they discovered that the power of that ownership could be multiplied many times by putting it anonymously in the name of an entirely new juridical person, such as a corporation.

When laborers first got together to help each other or protest, the form it took was probably that of a loose group getting together and discussing, and then perhaps sending a few representatives to the king or landlord to present their views or requests. Later there were guilds, and then labor groups within individual companies. Gradually the huge, powerful labor unions were formed.

Struggle or demand for change may have taken the form of simple unrest in the early periods of organization. It gradually took the form of refusal to send in their harvest, eventually even riots, and later the form of struggle evolved into votes, organized strikes, lockouts, boycotts and similar forms.

That was the old paradigm. If we just look at the evolution of organization superficially, it seems that we just had a lot of distinct, disconnected examples. If we look carefully, however, we see the pattern or structure underlying it.

If we are conscious of this process of algo-paradigm evolution, we sense what is going to happen as we move into the twenty-first century. In the new paradigm, the old algo-net forms will dissolve and be transformed into a living network. The enterprises and organizations of the future will be totally liberated. There will be no ownership, so there will be no need for any forms of ownership. There will be no labor, so there will be no need for any forms of labor organization. There will be no struggle, so there will be no need for a form in which it can express itself. These forms, which arose as catalyst adaptations useful for altering the world and preparing it for the next stage of beings, will soon be disappearing.

Today the advanced countries like America, Japan and several nations of Europe are at the last algo-net stage of administrative organization and moving on into the next live-net phase. The developing countries are still moving along at the stage of anima, idea, and so on. The breakdown of administrative society in the advanced countries (thanks to us human catalysts), and the evidence that these countries are in some initial process of building up a radical new organizational synthesis, show that we are now moving into the new phase. As new live-net organizations arise with less concrete structures or forms and eventually with no structures or forms, phenomena such as the Internet, many more people will be like the algo-net people which companies and organizations have on their hands today — feeling disorganized, afraid to move ahead, wanting to clutch on to the familiar past.

If we want to make the transition effectively and painlessly, it will be necessary for us to grasp one principle that is already guiding the evolving organizational life of the new era. This principle is abandonment or total entrustment.

An example to illustrate how total entrustment works is what happened when instead of old, direct, face-to-face exchanges, we began to use a medium such as plastic cards (credit cards and the like) to buy and sell, communicate information, and perform other transactions. The card plays an important role in feedback. When we wish to transfer information today, we have, besides a sender and a receiver, a card that functions as an agent in the process, enabling the feedback cycle to begin. How? Unless certain information from the sender and the receiver is exchanged, we can't have a transaction service. The card's role is to initiate and facilitate the information feedback cycle. If we want this or that kind of service we have to give out some information about ourselves to the other party or we don't get our card or the service. The card, therefore, results in the breakdown of privacy for the sender. Privacy is sacrificed within the domain of the card.

This is so, however, not only for the consumer who requests the service through the card, but also for the supplier who must provide information about the assets and kinds of services he or she can offer. The function of the card itself includes information, so this information now becomes open to the public. Therefore, the card becomes a medium with binding power to mutually penetrate and open up certain aspects of the privacy of the consumer and the supplier to each other and to the public. Organizations can no longer be formed without accepting this, which is why we call this state total entrustment. Unless we completely trust others, unless we reveal ourselves to others, we cannot mutually buy or sell — avail ourselves of others' services or have our services used.

How we can come to completely trust others will be clarified as we go along. However, it presumes that people will have evolved to the point where mutual trust is possible — the post-catalyst new beings — for this kind of trust has obviously not been part of the picture in algo-net society thus far. Yet, the old catalyst society is phasing out in favor of a direction toward greater mutual entrustment. This is why I say that instead of moving toward an information society, we are going into an era of entrustment, moving toward a total entrustment society.

In this stage, besides gradually weaning us from our deep-seated insistence on privacy, the old, ingrained mind-set of ownership will also be challenged. There was an article in the *Asahi* newspaper about a computer hacker in the United States. This hacker was trying to do away with copyrights. He felt it his mission to find good programs everyone can use, come up with improvements on them and then circulate them for free. He took pride in doing so.

This is, I believe, an example of the kind of intuitive behavior characteristic of the coming age. There are now people with the intuitive realization that we have already begun to move into an era of total entrustment. Now, rather than being worried about information leaks, we have to make all information public if we are going to come up with live systems — systems that meet the needs of the entire cosmic organism of which we are an integral part. In the era of total entrustment we will not only be creating viruses to break down old ways, but we will forsee the society to come. The karma (deep-seated, imbalanced habit or inclination) of ownership will be broken and the concept of work will vanish. That hacker will not be engaged in work, not even intellectual work, since he is doing his part for free. Strange, isn't it? People will make wonderful programs one after another for free and circulate them for free. Naturally, traditional economic principles and principles governing organizations and enterprises will also vanish.

Sounds too idealistic? Yes, for those who clutch on to playing the old algo-net games. Not for the new beings coming on the scene today, however. They already have this new mind-set and are following new play guidelines coming from our Space-Body Consciousness, which is the Great Producer/Director of it all. The ectoplasms who make up the new beings have a new set of costume and makeup instructions. A whole new play is taking shape in our Consciousness. We have only to wake up to it.

We were supposed to be money-minded in the past. We were catalysts. That role, however, is being wound down now. An impulse from the earth, out of the universe, is telling us we no longer have to play this game. Soon we will have no need of economy or money. The karma (imbalanced inclination) toward ownership will be broken, the concept of work will vanish, and our traditional monetary and business mentality will become passé and irrelevant.

The talk these days in America and the other advanced or powerful countries of the world is all about economics and the economy — how to end worldwide recession, how to improve the outlook for jobs, security, purchasing power, free trade and international markets. In other words, everyone wants money! What this means, obviously is that a great number of people still believe that money is the most important factor determing our future; that economic factors such as the capitalist system, free trade, consumer confidence, jobs and having money for living, health, retirement and old age, are the keys to our happiness and our future.

The definition of human beings as catalysts, however, makes it clear that no matter how much the economy develops (even if we can extend the benefits of capitalism to all the poorest countries of the world), its usefulness is limited. Making money will not bring us satisfaction. It was a clever carrot held out before us. The prospect of making money and having the power and material goods it could provide, successfully enticed us to do all the hard work necessary in the role of catalyst to prepare the world for the next stage of evolution.

We know in our hearts, however, that wealth is a mirage. Money can't produce the really big things like life, the earth's ecosystem, nature in its original state, the living system called Earth or any of the functions stemming from it, because money and economic activities are catalyst creations. The only thing money or economic activity can do is be a catalyst, decomposing and recomposing the continuum of life within earth's ecosystem. This includes the human body. Money and the economy can only work within the limits of their role as catalysts, and since that role is coming to an end, these have no future. We cannot place our confidence in them to help us as living beings. Those may seem like ominous statements, but by now perhaps, we are beginning to realize that they needn't bother us. We were supposed to be money-minded in the past. We were catalysts. That role, however, is being wound down now. An impulse from the earth, out of the universe, is telling us we no longer have to play this game. Soon we will have no need of economy or money. Realization of this point is extremely important.

As I pointed out at the end of last chapter, the karma (imbalanced inclination) toward ownership will be broken, the concept of work will vanish, and our traditional monetary and business mentality will become passé and irrelevant.

This becomes clear when we look carefully at money. Money, which represents value, has two big roles. One is as a symbol of ownership, the other as a symbol of exchange. Owners exchange it among themselves. So making money has basically been an economic game to effectuate ownership and exchange. This state of affairs is a typical end-result of humans having tread the road of life as individuals rather than as fully connected beings. Our present-day enterprise and industrial society has been trying to live solely on the basis of this economic principle of the centrality of money, individual ownership, economy and the goal of amassing personal wealth. It was a very narrow way of operating. When there are so many directions in which life could have developed, to limit ourselves to one game principle, to the narrow confines of money as the value in life, has been a challenge. Now, however, cosmic common sense seems to be undergoing a change and experiencing a recovery.

In the beginning, the framework in which money and economy would work was not very clear, so the range of life which economy dominated was small. However, it gradually began to exert its influence over an ever expanding number of human lives until it became global and even led to destruction of the environment. In other words, it is economic principle (money-mindedness) that has altered the environment irrevocably. The role of catalyst has been played out to its intended end. Adherence to economic principle was a typical outcome of individualism. The object of this action on the environment, however, was designed to pave the way for the next stage of evolution, not to destroy it completely. So the Life Force is saying to (Itself) us humans: That's enough now. You did well, but don't go on or you'll go too far.

Supposing a doctor were to go inside a human body and effectively isolate each of the organs, so that there was no longer any viable interface between them, or at most it became necessary for each to negotiate what it needed from the other organs to live. The heart would have to purchase oxygen from the lungs. The excretion system would charge exorbitant fees for its work of waste disposal. That is what we catalyst ectoplasms (humans) did to the body of the earth, all as part of the overall strategy of stimulating the earth-body into making adaptations.

At this time when we seem more absorbed than ever in worry over money and finances, it may seem unrealistic to say it, but soon we should find this all-preoccupying hold of money and economy on our thinking beginning to disappear. From now on we will begin to see the phenomenon of money and economic principle gradually dissolving. If ownership disappears, what need will there be for money? Unless we are getting this message clearly, we will be unable to fit ourseves into the concretely shifting world of tomorrow.

Since the first medium of exchange was born out of transactions between owners, currency was probably in the form of actual goods. That was barter. Fabrics such as silk were popular because they were easily transportable, whereas perishable goods did not serve as well. So, to start with, the currency of exchange was something like fabric, then stones and shells like cowry shells, then precious stones and metals like gold and silver. The concept of currency was after all the embodiment of ownership and exchange: currency in the form of actual goods, and then money in the form of metal coins, and later paper.

During this time the meaning of money changed. What was first used as currency was something actually useable, in itself a tool for living. That was the concept behind barter as money. At the stage of coins and paper, money used for exchange became a kind of bond or bill. The concept of money had changed to that extent — from actual goods, to precious metals, to trust, in terms of agreement as to value.

In the process of change, our sense of the value of money also changed. At the beginning, transactions could be carried out with objects visible right there to our very eyes. When the medium of exchange switched to metals and paper, the concept of ownership and exchange could be shifted into abstract space, since ownership and exchange could be simulated. The switch in form from concrete, actual objects to pieces of metal and bills was symbolic of and went hand in hand with many other shifts into abstract simulated space. As a result, social organizations could also be abstract, simulated beings. This is where enterprises began. Nations too became abstract, simulated beings — spaces with imaginary boundaries. Simulating an object of exchange by a piece of metal or a piece of paper was one of the most significant changes we humans ever made.

Since metal money did not deteriorate, we could always buy things as long as we had the metal money. We could even arrange to purchase something that was not there yet. Besides an actual goods economy, we now had a futures economy as well, enabling us to arrange for procurement of actual goods that would become available only in the future. What came on the scene next was the trust economy, enabling us to set up various options should certain actual goods not become available in the future. We later came up with options in commodity and stock exchange.

Upon reflection, money was originally a statement of individual rights, gradually evolving to give those rights concrete expression. If, before long, individual rights become indistinguishable and are replaced by a living network, money will obviously lose its original rationale. Instead of being a symbol of transaction between individuals, money will serve as a function of the network. The fundamental concept of money will have changed.

Whatever its use, money could not be clearly defined except in relation to the situations of individuals. This state of things is changing, however. Now methods of production are no longer limited to what one individual can accomplish, but have expanded to mass production by methods involving many people. In the era of live-net production, we will not be able to distinguish this person's work and that person's work. Clearly defining the contribution of specific individuals will no longer be possible or necessary in live-net production, information transmission, circulation or distribution. Copyrights and other such algo-net claims to fame and fortune will become irrelevant and counterproductive. Even in the matter of consumption, there will be no individual consumers, as new beings with increased proportions of ectoplasm and full cosmic consciousness take the place of old, algo-net individual-minded humans. All will change as we realize our connection to the living, cosmic network of Life and Consciousness.

These days we hear more and more people — in private life, business and even politics — saying that money is our biggest problem. This is an impulse coming from our universe consciousness. The universe is winding down the role of the human catalyst. We love money but at the same time fear it. We are mesmerized by it. Almost every move we make is dictated by it. We think we can't get away from it, can't live without it. These are catalyst feelings. In the period of transition, money will serve as a lever controlling the algo-net, but its meaning will change rapidly and in the end will be transformed and disappear. If we can understand this, we will be able to let go and have a calm attitude toward money as only a function or a tool during the transition. Money is the most typical of all the catalyst tools; it will be especially so in the period of transition. After all, however, money is nothing more than a catalyst. It is not the kind of thing to pour our life into, to identify with or put our hopes in.

We already know, for example, money cannot buy a person's love, because love is that person's real, honest feeling. So, no matter how much money we put out, we cannot really gain another's real, honest heart. Money eventually becomes powerless. Of course we can earn a lot of money and triumph over others, and people have a foolish tendency to judge people and things on the basis of wealth. But there is still something in us that holds back from bowing down completely to money. The world that money can command is limited. It appears to be all-powerful, but more and more of us will be waking up and seeing it in perspective.

Thus far, the number of people living as catalysts according to algo-net values has been the majority. That is why money could help one dominate in the deceptive world of appearances — of self and civilization. However, now, when self and civilization are crumbling, and true, honest feelings are coming to the surface, money is going to become more and more powerless. We will see that money, like science and technology, is only a catalyst. It is not a real part of the world of life. Even where society seems to be developed by means of money, we'll see that the development is unsatisfying, because it is disconnected with the life of the earth. More and more we will observe that people feel uncomfortable in such a space.

It is clear now that if the whole earth continues to experience the process of breakdown and reformation taking place at the hands of outsider catalysts, a new living network will be effected, bringing the earth closer and closer to a perfect live-net society. Money and the various organizations of human society have been the organic, living catalysts accomplishing this radical transformation. The time has already passed when money can be looked to as the thing that supports individual human rights, amplifies individual assets or ability, expands the sphere of a human's activities or domination, or serves as a means of achieving one's desires. Being unthinkingly bound to these passé ideas of money is what has put modern humans in a bind — modern humans with their deep concern about fundamental human rights and their intense pursuit of courses and therapies to achieve improvement or perfection as individuals. We are already shifting into a new age, an era of a new being, and even beyond. We will be fine without money.

This being the case, what will replace money? In his book *Power Shift*, Alvin Toffler pointed out that money (and the military which have been thus far the two most typical power bases) will break down and be replaced by information. However, I don't think it will be information of the type we talk about today, ordinary algo-net, scientifically and technologically created and transmitted information. When children nowadays use computers, they put something more than regular information into the equation. They plug in to the personal computer an information system that is different, a live-net type of information system — vitally linked to our real, full mind, the space Consciousness of our full universe-body. That is what we are dealing with here, information that is feedback from the live-net — Cosmic Life information.

The old kind of scientific and technologically created information is a relic of our catalyst past. Past? Seems hard to believe when we look around us today. It would appear that these power bases are still quite intact, still quite in control. To algo-net eyes, yes. If we look with live-net eyes, however, we can see all the signs of a cosmic coup d'état. The state of things is going to change dramatically.

Reviews of Our Long-running Sitcoms

We find ourselves now in a period of transition. Transition means change. To our human consciousness, all great changes on the earth so far have taken place over eons of time. Now, however, the pace of change is picking up and will apparently take place dramatically soon. In this period of transition, when we are no longer called upon to function as catalysts but expected to prepare for a new role in the Earth Story, what will it be like for us who are so conditioned to the life of catalysts?

Any period of change is felt differently by different types of people. To some, great changes are painful. They are especially difficult for those who are comfortable in their present situation. These types prefer the known, even if their comfort includes troubles, hardship and suffering. New ways of thinking and doing things do not come easily. There is resistance. To drag their feet, moan and make a fuss is part of the role these characters are playing. Such roles usually entail being phased out, and we can expect this eventuality to be the future for most of the characters in the present earth story. They will exit the stage as the various catalyst beings play out their role to its logical conclusion.

The all-absorbing health and healing drama, for example, will be playing itself out to its glorious end in a spiral of increasingly complex struggles between the major players — the doctors, the hospitals, the medical industry, the insurance companies and the lawyers (and, don't forget, Oriental medicine and the alternative, natural healers). At the same time the whole health and healing group, as well as the majority of humans who have participated in this drama as willing patients, will be faced with an array of increasingly severe illnesses that defy the best efforts, the most exhausting research of the best minds, and their most astounding technologies. The characters in the health and healing drama will struggle on a bit longer in a dramatic effort to figure out and control the impossible number of variables involved in the illnesses of the human body, relying solely on the power of the human brain. Left alone, the whole thing would no doubt eventually self-destruct, but it is due to be phased out of the picture by a new breed of beings who will refuse to get caught up in the drama of trying to deal with sickness by using their heads. We must admit, however, that the whole medical act has been very well played, and has furnished us with our fill of topflight drama.

Education has been another part of the drama occupying the stage for some time, and yet now finding itself being phased out. It served the whole catalyst purpose perfectly, absorbing major numbers of players in the process. It provided work for teachers, administrators, researchers, maintenance, cafeteria, coaching, counselling, and family liason personnel. It prepared generation after generation of young people to take their place in the ranks of catalyst workers, inculcating in them the formulas of thinking-human, ectoplasm strategy: think, use your head, study, trust in science and technology. Out of the schools came waves and waves of new experts and professionals, all motivated by dreams of fame and fortune to do the hard tasks of preparing the world to evolve further. It was brilliant. It is sad to watch the struggle now going on from lack of funds, lack of clarity about its purpose, confusion over methods, disbelief and despair over the new children coming onto the scene who no longer want to go to school, follow the courses, or take the adult world seriously.

The lawyers and the criminal justice system have given us some of our most gripping dramatic performances, and our most important support in the drive for individual rights, the cornerstone of catalyst life. Thanks to them, we were able to lose sight of the fact that we were essentially one, long enough for us to absorb ourselves in activities of good catalysts — breaking down the whole civilization we had so painstakingly built up. Here too, we have to hand it to the long line of willing clients who contributed priceless performances suing one another over every trifle imaginable, and letting the lawyers insinuate themselves and their exclusive language into even the most simple and what should have been do-it-yourself situations. The whole thing is now top-heavy with complexity, out of balance, despised and ready to be given a ceremonious boot.

Politicians and bureaucrats, even if we judge merely from the content of our nightly TV news shows, have played major roles in the drama of catalyst life. We take them so seriously that what they say and what they do are almost always front page, prime time information. They have done their part to carve up the world, the nations, the states, the cities and even the villages into disconnected, uncooperative mosaic pieces. Thanks to the situation they created, however, we were able to carry out the large-scale projects necessary to do the real work of breaking down the world. Without that atmosphere of disconnection and competition, effectively controlling or even cutting off the interaction of peoples, we would never have been able to kill each other or struggle for alternative methods of survival. But as it was, the body of human life was so traumatized that in the resulting struggle, we were able to do the trick of bringing ourselves to a point of readiness for evolution to a next stage — even in the so-called free and democratic countries.

Those in the money business did a class-A job in their roles. They created an atmosphere that totally absorbed their audience in its play. Perhaps nothing else on earth had such a hold on everyone as the emotions surrounding and evoked by the struggle to acquire and maintain wealth, and have the things money could buy — power, influence, material goods and so on — emotions nursed through the ages by those in business, banking, investments, and taxes.

The religious theme running through the whole play is another that cannot be left out. You have to hand it to them — how they were able to make themselves so important that they were considered indispensable, irreplaceable, and even infallible. The drama they furnished through competing doctrines — escalating the Crusades, the Inquisition, the age of Exploration, and lately even hit lists, sending off missionaries to foreign lands, developing churches, rituals, music. Did anyone do as much as them to further the cause of the catalyst task: work hard, sacrifice, don't complain, offer it up, trust you will get a reward, have lots of children, don't ask questions, believe blindly, trust in God, don't revolt or you will be punished forever in hell.

During this transition they find themselves still in business, for people feel more and more anxious, uneasy and afraid about certitudes, about the future, and life after death (which no one else but the researchers in the paranormal will say anything about these days). Yet fewer and fewer people really believe the old doctrines and the outdated morals. The leaders are either gallantly repeating and shoring up the traditional formulas, or milling around trying out various new rituals and activities to keep the interest of their followers.

Families, love and personal relationships fuel our soap operas with true-life stories of previously unmentionable topics for plays.

The family has contributed to the catalyst task like few other elements in the ectoplasmic strategy. They were the first line of the offensive, indoctrinating each new arrival on earth with all the tenets of the algo-net catalyst philosophy: use your head, think, work hard, make money, get a career, rule the world. Instead of maintaining the intuitive powers of space consciousness the children brought with them, parents humanized them by teaching them to speak — an ability which carried with it learning the adult, religious and cultural values of civilization. They plugged them into the religious system from birth, a system which insured that both parents and children would be kept locked into the ideas that would further the catalyst strategy of the ecto-plasms. Then at a certain agreed-on time (five years old), good parents loyally passed the children on to the educa-tion system where teachers would reinforce the lessons learned at home. During the transition now, the family is faced with its breakdown, just as it contributed to the breakdown of the world through the values it laid over each new child. Leaders of the algo-net try valiantly to prop up family values, but it is increasingly a losing battle — losing to something as yet unknown.

All of us actors and actresses on the stage of life have done a marvelous job of playing our part. We all find ourselves, however, on the verge of being out of work. The transition is a tough time, because we humans tend to see change as loss. We cling to the old and familiar.

It is, however, a time of excitement and possibilities for many others of us humans. We don't mind the coming change; in fact we look forward to an undreamt-of type of life with new and challenging roles. Many new actors and actresses are just coming on the scene to play these brand new parts. They are inexperienced and unsure of their roles. Without thinking, without even knowing they are different, they do what they feel the impulse to do. Like aristocrats after the French Revolution, we left-overs from a previous era find it hard to accept their behavior or understand what is in their heads.

Their new lifestyles, new ways of eating, sleeping and spending their time are simply a new form of play. The one Life underlying us all, the one same Consciousness that promotes this whole exciting concoction, has a new idea! As a result, we can expect a whole new set of characters and activities based on this completely different Consciousness.

It is important that none of us despair over the changes occuring in this transition period. We may want to continue on playing the same familiar games and make-believe. The fact seems to be, however, that when we came out to play today, there was the suggestion that we play something different and much more satisfying. Let's hear it out and see what it's going to be all about. After all, that is Consciousness, our real SELF deep down in us under this masquerade, wanting to change the play.

ONTOLOGY:
A NEW FOCUS

*While explorations of, or experience in
psychic and metaphysical power may seem
more spiritual than manufacturing automobiles, they will not do any better job of
taking us to the discovery of who or what
we really are.*

We come now to the part where we
have to deepen our level of consciousness about who we are. Through the
previous part of the book we have been
considering ourselves on the level of our
more obvious everyday consciousness
— considering the question of who we
are in the character role of the thinking-
human, the catalyst operating with only
partial consciousness. Hereon we will
change our focus to the question of the

who behind that character.

What was on the everyday minds of most of us in the previous part of the book was the breakdown occuring in the old familiar world around us. We wondered if there was a way to understand it. What is going on? Is it a usual or an unusual sign? Where is the breakdown going? Can we fix it or is it hopeless? What is going to happen to us and our world? What lies ahead in the twenty-first century?

A slightly different set of questions is on the mind of a significant other group of people. Many musicians, writers, young people and children feel estranged from ordinary culture, antagonistic toward adult algo-net values. They aren't aware of anything different about themselves. They express themselves without any particular consciousness that they are different. They just have different impulses and desires, which don't include any interest in what we adults would like them to accept and get used to for their own good, or for their happiness. They wonder what they can do to stop being bothered by parents, society, and sometimes police. Is there any adult out there who understands their consciousness, what is going on in their minds, who champions them, who would be able to take responsibility for giving them space to be fully themselves? Is there any voice who can express or formulate their consciousness and concerns?

The way to answer these questions and resolve our

fears and anxiety, we discovered, is not to go out and buy the latest bestseller explaining how we are to restore family and religious values, calm and control our rebellious youths, redefine education, revive the economy, straighten out the government, lawyers, insurance companies, and the health and military industries, improve ourselves through therapy or classes, and save the environment. The way to answer our questions and resolve our fears is to determine our identity more exactly, find out who and what we really are. We thought we learned a lot about ourselves when we discovered that we were catalysts working to prepare the world for evolution into the next stage. Now we're going to go a step deeper into the question of our identity. Or to put it a different way, we are going further out into space to view the human situation.

We already know that we are not to identify ourselves with the catalyst parts of ourselves — skills, intelligence and thinking, personality, science, technology and systems. What then are we to identify with? What is the "us" underlying and remaining through it all?

Answering this ultimate question of who we are is the concern of ontology. In ontology we focus on the deeper, more abstract questions about our reality. We saw in the last part of the book that it makes a difference whether we're entirely something out of nature or not. We'll see in this part of the book that it makes an even bigger difference whether we're physical and material only or also part spirit. If there is a spirit to us, we want to know what the nature of that existence is, and whether we are real or just a dream. Is there, in fact, any reality to our physical, material appearance? The answer to all these questions is what ontology is all about.

Ontology is also a way of perceiving things, a way that is different from the way of science. The way of science is to consider only what we can experience with our senses or with instruments — empirical evidence and data. It is a way of awakening to this world that we can see and hear and feel. The way of ontology uses intuitive evidence to consider what we suspect might exist or are almost sure exists but can't prove by empirical methods of science. It is a way of awakening to another world.

We are going to take the way of ontology. It is a way that will enable us to arrive at a final, satisfying understanding of who we really are. How can ascertaining our identity solve our concrete personal and world problems? How can this be more effective than analyzing our difficulties and coming up with concrete solutions? How this works, and how powerfully it works, will become very clear as we proceed.

Most of us have no memory of anything back beyond our childhood, if even that. Today, however, we are getting descriptions of details from the time of birth and even before. In some cases it may be because we never thought to ask very young children if they remembered anything back then. We presumed they didn't know anything until their brain developed. Some impulse, however, is leading us to inquire of them. Something is stirring in us, drawing our consciousness back to memories of a more original state. The time of our catalyst role is ending and we are being led to uncover something that we were unconscious of during that period. Children who have not been frightened into thinking they're crazy if they say what is on their minds are telling us things about life that are very jarring to our present mind-set.

It should not be a shock for us to find that these very young children speak of life back before birth into the physical human world, a life in which they do not think of themselves as humans. If we grew out of the universe, we also should remember what it was like. Why did we forget? How could this happen?

We were deluded. From the time we were born, we humans evolved under the illusion that we were getting to know things, gradually increasing our knowledge. The fact is that as we got to know some things we forgot (or were told to forget) other things — very, very important things. The net result was a loss of knowledge and a decrease in total amount of consciousness. That original, forgotten world — a world of infinite power and creativity — is what I am talking about when I say, the world of ontology. Recovering our memory of that world from which we really originate, and hence recovering the memory of who or what kind of being we really are, is what I call the way of ontology.

Some people seem to feel ontology is too difficult a word— too highfalutin'. If I say: "Ontology is distinguished from the material world of phenomenology," people think I am talking about outer space, removed from ordinary life as far as you can get. Actually, however, the world of ontology is accessible even if we have no education or experience. It is the world we grew out of and once lived happily in. If only we could remember. It is important that we think of ontology as being very natural to us, comfortably familiar, a world easily accessible to our consciousness, a world in which we had full consciousness.

Most of us wouldn't know what full consciousness is like, since we've always operated with only partial human consciousness characterized by thinking and painful learning. We've heard of saints and psychics having experiences of higher consciousness and powers of the mind beyond those that are normal for most of us humans, but little is yet known of it. Numerous people have had near-death experiences which suggest strongly to them that there is a kind of life that is quite different from present-day human life. So far, however, nothing clear has come out of these experiences for us to understand. Scholars have been working on the question of what is beyond "human" consciousness for years now, but most of them have been operating under the limitations of empirical, scientific method. Some people who have been exploring psychic and metaphysical levels of consciousness tend to think that we'll find it is nothing but ordinary knowledge — that our human brain power hasn't been fully tapped yet: "We're only using five percent of our brain power." Others think that access to psychic and metaphysical levels of consciousness is equivalent to knowing how to tap into the higher intelligence of spirits through channeling, astrology, tarot cards and the like. A few people have caught a glimpse of full consciousness through years of meditation or shortcuts with LSD. These experiences definitely change them but do not put them into a lasting state of full consciousness.

The full consciousness we are capable of goes way beyond these, and while explorations of, or experience in, psychic and metaphysical power may seem more spiritual than manufacturing automobiles, they will do no better job of taking us to the discovery of who or what we really are. In fact these efforts often inhibit the process, and may sometimes be very dangerous.

Why do I use the word ontology and not just consciousness? Because the answer to the question of how we access full consciousness does not come from long effort at trying to understand different levels, types or processes of knowing — i.e. consciousness. The ultimate answer to this question comes — Bang! — from a non-process of awakening to the final point of conscious awareness about who we are — ontology.

The world of ontology seems difficult because we have the feeling it cannot be entered except through the world of thought, of demanding, complicated exercises and fierce disciplines. "I have to join a class or go to Tibet for a year."

In this present era, we are being impelled to radical change, to dig up the roots, habits and traditions of the physical, material, phenomenological world of thinking, words and systems to rearrange and build something new. Even when told that it is better to do things spontaneously without thinking, most people react that this is not common sense. The commonly accepted position is that thought ranks highest and that people who don't think are not very highly developed. For these people there is probably no other way than to use some kind of thought (logic or argument) to convince them that they have been deluded about the importance of thinking and the material world. Thinking has to be put in its place and given a coup de grace by thought, and along with thinking, the absolute conviction we humans seem to have about matter and physical reality. This troubles modern humans, yet it has to be done. First, we'll deal with thinking.

I have called our present half-life "algo-net." It is characterized by a state in which people have no awareness of the continuity and connectedness of everything. We now sense everything piecemeal, as separate, cut off, isolated, like pieces of a mosaic. It is characterized by our slow, unsure, often erroneous processes of thought and reasoning, instead of the flawless direction of intuition we could have if we were connected to our home world of ontology.

To illustrate, suppose there is a tree. The tree is alive. A branch is growing out of the trunk. That branch is cut off and processed to make baskets, a chair, a little house. The stick and the things made out of it are now dead, cut off from the main trunk. They are algo-net, no matter how beautiful, intricate, or marvelous they have become. In terms of life, that stick and the things made out of it are nothing in contrast to a live branch, still one with the tree, in the living network of the tree — i.e., live-net.

Continuity and connectedness are characteristic of the live. Constant consciousness or awareness of our fundamental source, the world of ontology, the infinite tree of Life, is what connects us and makes us really alive. Without that we are dead, though we think we are alive. What we are talking about, then, is very simple.

Put a new-born baby in water. Almost without thinking (shall we say reflexively) the baby moves its arms and legs so as to get itself back up to the surface. The water is connected to cosmic life, so it is living — like the branch connected to the tree. It does not have to think in order to move, and those beings that are in it don't need to think either in order to know how to act in the water. Certain senses in the baby react to the energy and vibrations of the water. That is what the world of ontology is like. Everything is interconnected, responsive, knows just what to do, is perfectly taken care of. Interconnectedness and being joined to cosmic life is at the base of it all.

Later, however, when that baby is introduced to thinking, the swimming may not come easily at all. The baby has become cut off from that omniscient life source. It is now in our human world.

Everything in our adult human world is disconnected from the tree of life so to speak. Getting all wrapped up in the material world, concentrating our efforts on getting to know the physical world and its laws, has turned our attention and consciousness away from our original intuitive abilities. As intuition has dulled, we have let omniscient and omnipotent powers that were ours slip away. Our sciences and modern mosaic logic have pulled us farther away from our original state. We have now become riveted on what we can experience with our senses. We have now lost and forgotten the knack of responding and experiencing with full Consciousness. This all happened naturally because that was the way the Great Producer, (or the Great Playing Child) thought it up, to pave the way to the next stage of evolution in the Earth Story.

Where are things going today? They are going back to the way of connectedness with cosmic life, to live-net existence and society, to the way of ontology — full consciousness. Saying that ontology sounds so terribly profound and difficult indicates that we are still peasants in the world of logic, reasoning, and appearances. What difference does it make if we don't understand everything with our heads as long as we grasp things with our whole being. If we try to recover our connection to ultra Life and Consciousness by logic and reasoning, we'll find that it's impossible.

We modern humans try to use logic even to find love. How often does it work? No matter how strongly we believe two people ought to go together because logic says so, they often don't. Love is a vibration. It happens when two people resonate. Sometimes the conditions defy all logic. Likewise thinking and logic are useless in achieving live-net living. Unless we cut thinking in two with a sword, throw out everything thinking has made up and return to zero, to the point of nothingness or death, we will never be clear enough to recover awareness of our connection with cosmic life and hence to really live.

The true life world is a world of zero — zero meaning, zero judgements, zero values, zero logic, zero effort. All the titles, positions, degrees, values, powers, sciences, schools and systems we think make us something and others nothing are in complete contradiction to real life. Zero logic allows us to return to the Infinite Live, reconnects us with the sensitivity of Infinite Nature. When I say nothing equals infinity I mean that when thought is reduced to zero, we are linked to our point of origin — like the branch to the trunk of the tree. The world of ontology is simple. It is a world in which we can understand without thinking, where we can do things without thinking. In fact, without even trying. The moment we try to understand (evidence that we are operating on our own individual brain power rather than with the power of the full tree) we find ourselves with a problem. We have to study it.

So conditioned are we to the habit of thinking that even the very moment we are told ontology can be understood if we just don't try and don't reason, we start thinking! We think to ourselves: "What does that mean — 'We can understand without thinking?'" The habit of thinking has become so deeply ingrained in us! We are taught to think from an early age. We are taught to treasure thinking ability as the crowning glory of the human race.

Not to think is to throw open our consciousness in a childlike way. Once we acquire the habits associated with being adult however, it is difficult for consciousness to be open and expansive. The world of ontology seems difficult because we have the feeling it cannot be entered except through the world of thought, of demanding, complicated exercises and fierce disciplines. "I have to join a class or go to Tibet for a year." Actually there is nothing simpler than re-entering the world of ontology. Just turn off all human activity, return to the state of zero values, zero thinking, and you're in it! It is a world that is natural to us, a world that requires no thinking, no exercises, no difficult classes, no living in a monastery or on a mountaintop. In that world we can truly take it easy. We can do what we want and quit trying so hard. Then amazingly many things start working and coming together. We begin to have frequent experiences of synchronicity. We are just thinking of someone and they call us on the phone, or we want that parking space under the tree and when we get there the space opens up. However, we are so conditioned to our world of thinking, planning, controlling, and trying to cause effects, that we shrug off these meaningful coincidences. We are convinced that ontology, intuition, inspiration and telepathy exist at a difficult level of knowledge or ability, requiring difficult steps, training and practice to attain.

Looking at the hologram of this world and the play going on in it, I see that operating in the live-net form of existence seems to come much easier and more naturally to looked-down-on, unimportant, unthinking, simple ordinary people than to power players, intelligentia, pseudo-intellectuals, experts and successful people who work so hard to make themselves important. In our space Consciousness We thought up and played out these latter marvelous characters who are soon lured off by the attractions and temptations of the algo-net society they fashion and maintain. Things are going to change, however. Our space Consciousness is saying that it's time to end this act of the play. It's getting too complicated and absorbing. Not good for cosmic health!

I was recently looking at some meaningless cartoons. It occurred to me that such cartoons make us feel uneasy. We feel uneasy because we are put into a state in which we cannot think, a state in which thought doesn't work as usual, and it is thought, of course, that allows us to create meaning. The reaction to meaninglessness is a little different than the reaction one gets from drugs. The reaction to drugs is one of the mind and thoughts becoming high. In this state one is not bound by thoughts. In fact, the feeling is as though all thoughts have wings and fly away. In contrast, meaningless cartoons make our thoughts seem to become suddenly limp and drain away, so we feel more and more uneasy. Ultimately, however, when all our thoughts are gone, even uneasiness is gone, and since we are then in a world of no-thoughts, we return to the world of ontology. Therefore I think meaningless cartoons are a means of taking us back to the world of ontology. In that sense, they are close to Zen.

The koans, those short pithy riddle questions of Zen, like "What is the sound of one hand clapping?" serve the same function. Zen practice makes you go ahead and speak nonsense and in the end destroys thinking. If you are an adult, however, you feel you have no other way to deal with the koans than to keep on thinking about them. It is difficult for you to be convinced there is another way, unless you keep following your thoughts to a point where they fade away. That is what ascetic, religious and philosophical disciplines have been trying to do from ancient times. They attempt to control thought with thought, to transcend, ultimately, the influence of thought. It takes so much time, however! No one ever arrives at that point within their lifetime. So Zen tried to devise a way to do it quickly, to cut thought in two with a single stroke of the sword.

The two best known sects of Zen — Rinzai Zen and Soto Zen — show you how, though with slightly different approaches. Rinzai Zen uses logic and words in a sort of backhand fashion. They throw out all kinds of thoughts, then let the thoughts knock against each other until they disappear and the function of thinking ceases to work. This is how they escape from thought. The koans of Rinzai Zen are an escape from thought. They are effective and are simpler to use than other methods, and accomplish their work in a shorter time. Soto Zen does not even allow thoughts to come in. They just sit you down and don't even tell you what to do. At first, as you just sit there, you feel your legs ache and your body getting tired. Gradually, however, you don't feel even that and, in the end, all thought ceases. The two methods differ a little, but Zen is the most developed as regards ways to escape from the tyranny of thinking.

Zen comes close to ontology, but doesn't quite make it. Zen is still phenomenological ontology. Words belong to the world of phenomena and the world of logic. Forms are expressed by words, but space Consciousness, which has no form, cannot be expressed by words. Zen clearly starts from the world of forms:

first, controlling the body to escape from the body, then, with methods like the koan, controlling the mind to escape from the mind. Zen is the dead end of phenomenology. It butts physical and spiritual methods against each other and in doing so gets farther and farther away from their influence and finally overcomes them. This is not ontology, however, but phenomenology. The Zen people realize it, but hope that in the process they will, by some miracle, in some magic instant, be transported over the wall separating the two.

Why can't Zen make the jump? Because they think they have to jump. They think there is a wall, and someone or something, maybe nothing, over the wall. That is dualism. There is no other in ontology. No other world that is separate, different or distinct; only another world that is one and the same. Another reason Zen is not the answer is because practitioners of Zen use methods. You can put methods and systems into the same bag with words and thoughts and get rid of them. No method is necessary, as you will soon realize. The system of Zen requires long training. Yet, there is no guarantee that the long training will bring results. There are times when it does, and other times when it doesn't achieve anything. Many times people retreat and start over. All this going back and forth is not going to help you make it into the twenty-first century of ontology. There isn't enough time left to do it using these usual human ways.

The hologram and script of the play for humankind does appear, however, to have us going into an era when our daily lives will be ontological. (Actually we will be recovering that mode.) In other words, it has us going into an era when everything will be done in an open, spontaneous childlike way (not the adult, professsional, scientific, technological, expert, big-deal-but-unable-to-deliver way of the algo-net play). People in America are moving in that direction today. By means of various sense and perception simulations, virtual reality for example, they are reducing thought down to the level of sensation. With the energy whirling around these sensations people break through and recover their original consciousness. We must remember, however, that virtual reality has one danger: when people take off the glasses and gloves, they tend to think they are returning to real reality. Human life, however, is as much an illusion or make-believe as virtual reality.

We're already in a post-Zen stage. Zen still mixes thought and senses together and tries to make a breakthrough in a leap from the apparently real, appearances-only reality of phenomenal life, into the only real life — eternal, non-phenomenal life. What I am now going to guide you to is an easier way — a way that is surely occurring to other people as well because the impulse is coming out of our universe-body.

These days we are seeing, hearing and feeling numerous expressions of an impulse to lighten up in order to recover full consciousness. The whole world is resonating to this impulse. It's not only the noticeable breakups such as are occurring in Europe that are talking to us, however. Look at the fitness centers, spas, aerobic halls and jogging trails, for example. People trying to loosen up, to find ease from the burdens and dis-ease brought on by humanly-thought-up pressure, rules and expectations, the bombardment from algo-net advertising, government infringement and demands. Today there is clearly an impulse for all of the world to turn back toward the pleasant, easy, no-thinking, no-trying, spontaneous world of ontology.

Life in the next stage is to be characterized by a return to a live-net attitude — an awareness that everthing is alive and that everything is connected. It will be characterized by a profound respect for intuition rather than thinking; by authenticity, spontaneity and honest feelings, rather than learned behavior, rules, effort and artificiality; by sharing as one rather than by individual ownership and a money-based society; finally, by activities and products that are live.

How is this utopia to be achieved? Science and technology have tried but aren't succeeding. Religions have tried and been unsuccessful. Education has failed. Money-making has turned us into wrecks. Why? Because none of these activities was geared to achieve a utopia. They appeared to be so geared; we were definitely under the illusion that they were. Instead, however, they were catalyst activities we carried out under the direction of ectoplasm. They were constructs of the human mind. Their purpose, unknown to us, was to lead us into activity that would break down certain elements of the world in order to prepare for a new stage of evolution.

The way of ontology is the way of no-thinking. And please be very clear about this point: by no-thinking we're not just talking about quieting the mind for a few minutes during relaxation or meditation. We're talking, literally, about no more thinking, no longer turning to our brain, our imagination, our memory, logic, reasoning, cause and effect for help. Instead of saying, "Think!" we say, "Don't think!" No more trying to figure out why something is happening or what we should do. No more judging — something we're doing almost every waking moment of the day: This is good, that is bad. I like this, I hate that. He is stupid, that plan is great. She is ugly, she's a dream. Isn't this weather terrible? What a beautiful morning! This country's going to pot. We're the greatest in the world! If we just open our whole being, and get used to being without all the static from our human minds, we begin to realize that the information is all there, all ready for us. We notice that a perfectly wonderful operating system is already in place, needing no help from us. No effort, no trying. Everything we need has been there all along but we were just too absorbed in the thinking play to notice it. The time has come to go back and pick up where we started — making up something to play. Utopia is to be achieved through a simple awakening of our consciousness.

The basis of thought, motion and the self is not in the body. It is clearly in space — empty space or nothingness (to speak phenomenologically), pure Consciousness (to speak ontologically). So, ultimately there is no phenomenology, no material world. It is gone — or rather is smashed. It does not exist.

We saw in an earlier chapter how strongly we are being held in the grip of phenomenology — a mind-set that insists on accepting the material, observable world as the real world. To lay the way open for even a consideration of the possibility that anything beyond the physical exists, we need to address this question of the reality of the material world.

As I mentioned in the last chapter, today we are being impelled to radical change, to dig up the roots, habits and traditions of the physical, material, phenomenological world of thinking, words and systems to rearrange and build something new. For people anchored in the material, phenomenal world there is probably no other way than to use some kind of phenomenal method to convince them that they have been deluded about the importance of the material world. The absolute, unshaken conviction we humans seem to have about matter and physical reality has, like thinking, to be put in its place and given a *coup de grace.*

There are various methods we could use, but one method is reconstructing the past, going back upstream to childhood and beyond. This method is called retrospection — a methodology of phenomenological ontology. Computer graphics has made it possible to illustrate quite well the path of evolution from present-day humankind back to the beginning of the physical universe. Such a tape would sell well because it would be equivalent to the most fantastic dream ever dreamed. One look at it and we would understand everything. We have arrived at a time when the world of ontology can be seen with our eyes! We will follow that path all the way back and see what there was at the beginning.

As if replaying the film or dream of life in reverse, we go back to childhood, to infancy, to the stage when we were a fetus or embryo. Even then, however, we have not retraced the path completely. From the embryo we go back to our parents and back further to ancestors. What happens even farther back? There is no more trace of humans and we are in a world of tiny little monkeys. Before that we were not mammals, but reptiles, batrachians, fish, protozoans and finally bacteria and amoeba. Farther and farther back upstream we were organisms with only a nucleus, like viruses. Further back that strain disappears and we were organisms like coacervate, like waterdrops floating on the ocean. Farther back, even that disappears and there were only planets. Then even the earth disappears leaving only a primitive solar system. Next even the sun disappears and there is only gas, clouds of elementary particles, and back until finally there is nothing.

How could nothing have such power over us today? There was nothing in the universe to begin with, so logically there should still be nothing there today. Nothing comes from nothing. Yet we continue to think according to the logic of those who came onto the scene later, in scientific times. We think we see, hear and feel a universe full of things. They are, however, after all only appearances, illusion. Nothing is there. Only space. The only real reality is consciousness, our consciousness, Pure unembodied Consciousness and the dreams and dramas in our infinite Consciousness. As humans we think there have to be logic and laws, yet when there was nothing, there was no logic and there were no laws.

Obstetricians are now beginning to report that infants in their mothers' wombs have dreamt the dream of millions of years of evolution before being born. Fetuses are not unconscious. They have gone through all the waves of evolution organisms go through from single-cells, like amoeba, to the beings of today. They have literally dreamt all the sensations and conceptions that have taken place during that process of evolution. At birth, babies often have the faces of old men or women. They have dreamt a dream of several million years before being born, so no wonder they look this way. Of course there is also the shock of being born, of coming out of the womb into this world. If we truly sense the being of a newborn infant, we sense a depth within that being that goes beyond human understanding. Soon, however, the baby forgets the dream of origins and plays the part of a baby.

We can say, therefore, that adulthood is a period of existence during which we have lost the memory of our several-million-year evolutionary dream. We try to substitute for it with thought. That dream of several million years' evolution contains in it all wisdom. Since babies have seen every possible situation, they have the big picture. With this perspective, the concerns of humanity today are not really central issues. The environment, depleting the ozone, running out of oil, Westernizing the whole world, the disappearance of democracy, the length of people's hair, the color of their skin, artificial boundaries portioning up the earth....We are bogged down in issues that are irrelevant to Life itself. Babies remember from having seen the whole picture. As they grow up and take on the biases of adults around them, they forget all this previous part of the dream. We resulting adults have it in our subconscious, but it is covered over. We seem to have forgotten our essential connection to the cosmos.

As human adults we make all kinds of commodities and provide all kinds of services to satisfy our needs. These needs are all on the surface level of consciousness. We are not conscious of our real, deep needs. These days, however, we are seeing the appearance of things like dream machines. A few years ago we had those flotation tanks in which you float on salt water in a tank pitch black and devoid of all sound — like being deep in the universe. Such phenomena I think indicate an urge to return to the world of that several-million-year dream.

Utilizing retrospection, a tool of phenomenological ontology, is one way to re-experience that dream and then go back beyond it to our original state. Another way, although it may sound like I'm contradicting myself utilizing something I criticize so much, is to use the logic of science. (You will understand soon, however, the method in my madness. It's a little dirty since it will enable me to let good old catalyst science dig its own grave.) Using the retrospective method, a science called cytology or cellular biology found that the skin, bones, organs and tissues of the human are formed out of cells. The human body and mind grew out of the mechanism of physiological exchanges among cells. The frontier was moved back farther by molecular biology. Cells are made of molecules. Logic impelled scientists to look even deeper. What were molecules made of? Atoms. What was inside atoms? The quest took them back to the world of elementary particles. At this point, physics took over and went back to the origin of elementary particles — the world of quarks, leptons and bosons. Actually it is not clear whether the quark is an elementary particle or not. At any rate, this is the way they traced life all the way back.

As we go back like this, laws simplify. According to scientists, it is evident that the laws of elementary particles stem from combinations of elementary particle laws at the very root of life. These combinations then became the laws of cells, and in turn, a combination of the laws of cell-thought and cell-action became the laws of humans — human biology and psychology. This process is called reductionism — explaining complex phenomena or structures by relatively simple principles, as by asserting that life processes are instances of chemical and physical laws.

Reductionism takes us all the way back to the world of elementary particles. However, when reductionism comes to its limits, and the logic of phenomenological ontology takes us the rest of the way back to our origins, we realize that the laws at the very point of origin, when thrown up against each other, disappear. When a particle and an anti-particle are thrown against each other they vanish, according to the law — plus, minus = zero — and return to space. At this point, scientists are stuck. Since the particles are reduced to space, they have to admit space, but science starts from the premise that there is nothing in space. How can matter come out of space — out of nothing (zero) — let alone spiritual and physical phenomena including humans and the human mind? The universe is not a mechanical collection of individual parts or particles.

We have attempted to use logic to go back upstream to the origin of the universe, but several things have to be said about logic. There are several contradictions possible in logic. One is reduction to absurdity, which takes you along the way of thought according to science and knowledge only to find that you are involved in a contradiction, or that your argument simply disappears. Hideki Yukawa, Japan's first Nobel prize winner in physics, said that the logic of the material system leads to the theory of elementary particles but that if you go back farther, the laws of physics disappear; in fact, the laws of science disappear. You reach a point of nothing.

Kurt Godel said that mathematics is more strictly science than physics. He tried to determine through axioms and theorems — the basic logic of mathematics — whether or not the mathematical system was applicable or contradictory to the universe. Whitehead and Bertrand Russell completed the work on mathematical principles, calling their work Principia Mathematica. It is the most fundamental work we have today, vying with Newton's principles of physics. Using the Whitehead and Russell principles, Godel found he could not prove, nor could the strictest mathematics prove, that the mathematical system was applicable to the origin of the universe. His finding is referred to as Godel's Theory of Impossibility. The fact that even mathematics cannot account for the origin of the physical universe suggests that the most basic laws of science such as those of physics are inadequate to answer the question of the true nature of the universe.

A Canadian neurosurgeon named Wilder Penfield devised an experiment to look for the nucleus of the human self — that which makes the human human — in the brain. He found, however, that there was no such nucleus anywhere in the brain. He came to the conclusion that the origin of judgments about who we are and what controls all our actions is not in the brain. All this must come from outside us.

It is from space that the driving force, the motive power behind and energy source of all apparent motions, action and reaction comes. In the apparent nothingness of space is the fullness of being — pure, infinite, unembodied Consciousness.

Now, in space Consciousness there is no cause and effect relationship. So we must conclude that since it appears all reactions or motions in this phenomenal world — whether they be of muscles or machinery — are physical motions, the driving force or the moving power behind every basic physical or chemical reaction is space Consciousness itself, which has no cause and effect relationship. How do we deal with this? Scientists still have no answer.

This is very similar to the case of Penfield. If the basis of thought and of the self is not in the body, then it is clearly in space. Penfield had to conclude, in spite of himself, that space Consciousness is the mind, and the brain its consignment circulation center or transistor. Being a scientist he resisted coming to that conclusion. Hiroshi Shimizu, a professor of pharmacology at Tokyo University, also came unwillingly to the conclusion that the motive power behind all physical systems (the human body belongs to the physical system of organic physics) was space. He concluded that the motive power behind both the mind and the body was space — empty space, nothingness (to speak phenomenologically), full space, infinity, pure Consciousness (to speak ontologically). So in the end, phenomenology is gone — or rather is smashed — here. Thus Yukawa's saying that laws no longer apply, and Godel being forced to proffer his Theory of Impossibility.

We now have a substantial body of evidence that phenomenology cannot stand on its own and that science is inadequate to the task of determining the origin of the universe. Many professional scientists know this to be the case but are afraid to acknowledge it for fear of losing their authority. The situation is very much like the one into which these modern scientists put the theologians back in the Middle Ages. Now it's the scientists who are on the hot seat pooh-poohing the incontestable in order to protect their turf. This is an age of de-modernization. Modern scientific logic is breaking down at its roots.

Just as science is at a loss when it comes to the point of breaking through phenomenology, many other fields are at a loss. We see politicians stuck to make old tried and true techniques work as today's political world breaks down. The military have found the logically ultimate threat — nuclear might — unworkable. Just as science breaks down in the face of ultimate ontology, so too does politics. Looking at the present situation we can say that economic power will have reached its limits soon. We already see clear signs of this.

Money too. Supposing you make a lot of money. Say you make several billion dollars, several thousand billion, several thousand billion times several thousand billion. At first you are powerful. Take it to its limits, however, and your money-making becomes meaningless. At a certain point the money is no longer useful as capital or as purchasing power. As you become richer, the number of poor increases. The more you gain, the less purchasing power others have. Ultimately, since you have all the money, no one else has power to buy anything from you, so you can't make any more money, and neither can others make anything for you to purchase with your wealth. When money-making reaches its ultimate limits, its effectiveness disappears. Just as having the ultimate military power is useless, so too is having ultimate monetary power. In the end we realize that they are all form and no substance, no reality, nothing. We are now close to arriving at this state.

As we look honestly at reality all around us, we begin to see the cracks in the seemingly solid, indestructible mass we call phenomena. It looks to us like there are people and things out there around us. It also sounds like it, smells like it, tastes like it, and feels like it. In reality, however, all this is illusion. How do we explain it? What is the reality behind the illusion? What is the reality behind us?

We must now answer for ourselves the ultimate question of life: Who are we? Are we just humans? The answer to this question is going to satisfy our curiosity about our identity and also about all the other questions we have of life: Is there a God? How did the world and humans originate? What was the purpose of earth and human life? Are they real or not? What is going to happen in the future?

We come now to that final point of understanding who we are. In that understanding is complete knowledge of all there is to know.

The answers to the ultimate questions of our identity and of life have eluded us through the ages of human life. They have been a mystery to religion, an enigma to philosophy and an impossibility for science. Everywhere we've turned we've come up against a wall or a thick door, unable to get through or across. What is on the other side? This is the wondering feeling we humans have had in our collective mind for centuries.

That, however, is precisely the problem. Asking such questions is a clear giveaway that we're using our heads. If we do so, if we use our human minds to answer these questions of our identity and of life, we will always run up against an impenetrable barrier, because the human mind is anchored in the phenomenal, material, physical world. It thrives on process. It makes up the wall! It doesn't know how to operate in any other way, any other medium, any other mode, any other milieu.

Full Consciousness is not something to be shown, illustrated, argued to or proven. It is something you are just aware of, or you aren't. There is no process. Moving from our present phenomenal state of consciousness to the non-phenomenal is like waking up.

When you are asleep and dreaming, you are simply aware somehow of lots of images and occurrences, many of them bizarre. You don't think to yourself: "I am asleep. How can I get to the state of awakeness? What is it like on that 'other side'?" No, you are simply either asleep or awake. When you awaken, you are aware that you were sleeping and dreaming, but you don't say to yourself: "Oh, now I understand what being 'awake' is like." You take that for granted. All you think to yourself is: "Oh, I was asleep. I was dreaming. Now I'm awake."

That is the situation we're in now. As humans, we're asleep and dreaming away. That is in fact the ground of another definition of the human. The human state is full Consciousness in a sort of sleep, a state of awareness in which the consciousness is so focused on particular imaginings or dream-like fantasies that it is absorbed momentarily in this play. It is mesmerized to the point of forgetting the reality of the situation. This absorption results in partial consciousness which we label "human." What we are seeing is often bizarre enough, but we don't need to get all philosophical and scholarly about it and sweat over such questions as "What is it like to be awake? How can I get from this state of sleep to the state of being awake? How can I get from partial consciousness to full Consciousness?" All we do is just sleep on or fantasize on until we wake up or snap out of it. When we do, we'll realize we were asleep or daydreaming and feel we are again in our normal waking state of full consciousness. That's all.

So we need not fret; we need not worry; we need not get excited; we need not be anxious for answers and explanations. We are simply asleep or daydreaming. We can relax and take it easy. We can sleep on or play on. We'll wake up at one time or another. When we wake up again, we'll feel we're awake.

In this human, dream-like play we know what the feeling of being awake is like: It is awareness, clarity, a sharp, clearheaded feeling that "I am awake. This is reality." That is the way we will feel when we awaken or snap back to our full Consciousness. Right now we as humans are experiencing awakeness within awakeness.

There is, however, a problem of how to talk about it. In the human state, we depend on thoughts and words to express ourselves, to understand and make ourselves understood. Understanding implies or depends on information coming in from outside of us. For reasons we will soon see, however, in the unseen world of ontology, thinking and words are unnecessary. In the world of ontology there is actually no thinking; there is only awareness or consciousness, which does not come to us but is just there through immediate, comprehensive grasp or intuition. In that state we do not go through a process of arriving at it. It is impossible, therefore, to fully understand unseen, unheard, untouchable reality, with human thoughts, or to describe it with human words.

How do we re-create the beauty of a sunset, or the magnificence of a field of daisies for one who has no sight? How do we communicate the aromas of apple, orange, lilac or heather to one who has no sense of smell? We try to describe them with words, but the results are totally unsatisfactory. We can't. Words just don't do it.

We can try desperately to communicate some feel for our unseen world by thoughts and words, but the problem is accentuated by the English language. English reflects an approach to life that is very individualist, separatist and divisional. It distinguishes between so many subjects, between present and past, between animate and inanimate, and between genders. Language is a good example of catalyst activity. We humans use it under the illusion that the more we develop it, the more brilliantly we are evolved. In reality, the more categories and distinctions we make up, the farther we get from reality, which is interconnected unity, a living network. English reflects our situation: we now have no way to express unity, because we don't even recognize it any more. In writing this book, I am faced with the daunting task of using words to describe a reality that cannot be described through words, only known as experienced directly.

If we can't derive the pleasures of understanding the unseen, unheard, unfelt world from words and thoughts, how do we do it? Return to our natural setting. Have no thoughts. Then it is very simple, we just grasp it. The way back to our natural setting is to break away from words and thoughts and simply open fully and resonate. That is why I have insisted on not getting hung up on words. It may be somewhat shocking, therefore, to read the following in words, but if you just let the words flow through you, read them with no thoughts, your intuitive powers open wide, it will all fit together without your laboring over it. You will find yourself saying, "I wouldn't know how to explain it but somehow I 'feel' it." Don't let the words deter you then. In the following passage is the answer to your ultimate question — and mine — to our ultimate question:

忧

Who am I?

- I am pure unembodied Consciousness existing without beginning or end in infinite space.
- I am infinite nothingness and yet I am infinite everything for I am the original creator of images like the sun and planets, plants, animals and humans, and the life force behind their imaginary activities. They have being, but only in my mind as part of Me.
- I am not a separate supreme being who is creator and master of a lot of separate inferior beings out there in a physical, material world. There is no such God for there are no such separately existing creatures. There is only Me, pure unembodied Consciousness, and the images and dramas I play out in my mind. They are all my play. They have no other reality or purpose. They are only there in the eternal now of my mind.

Being infinite consciousness, it is my nature to be a making-up, imagining, daydreaming, creating-ideas being. Billions of worlds, systems, characters and events fill my mind, flow through my mind, in an unbeginning/unending stream of consciousness, all in an infinite now. I think of myself as a child who, having no one else nor anything else to play with, spends its time forever playing make-believe.

One of those billions of scenarios I made up is what I could call the "Earth Story." I made up a world to operate in a cause-and-effect environment, with developments taking place by way of evolution. Being a precocious child, I put a very creative twist on the thing, however. I imagined it as a hologram. That way, although it seemed to Me like I was doing things in time and space, actually it was all there in my eternal now.

I first imagined clouds of nebulous gas, which collected as solids, blew up and split into millions of galaxies of stars. Through one star I gave rise to planets, and on one of them, which I called "earth," I thought up quite a drama in which I became various evolving creatures, changing the scenery from time to time through the action of numerous catalyst characters which I played in my mind. I even came up with another very interesting development — of having a being from another dimension (called ectoplasm) come into the "Earth Story" and take up life inside of upright-walking primates. To these hybrid creatures I gave the name of "humans."

Humans, then, are characters in my Consciousness, like fingers and toes that a creative child can bring to life in some sort of puppet game or play. When as human I look out of the human body, I see my nose, fingers and toes as distinguishable shapes and note that each performs a different function. They are obviously, however, connected to my play human body. They do not exist separately.

In the Earth Story I imagined bodies within bodies within bodies. Looking inside myself, I am the all-enveloping consciousness-body, supporting and sustaining countless energy-bodies inside, which in turn permeate and envelop individual solid-bodies of various shapes and forms. A "triple body," as it were. (I imagined something even more fascinating, because looking inside the human there are numerous smaller and smaller bodies such as organs, tissues, cells, molecules, atoms and particles, each a kind of body with its own level of activity and consciousness, each enveloping those smaller than itself. And looking outside the human there are numerous larger and larger bodies, the earth, other planets, suns and galaxies.) Bodies within bodies, within bodies, all interconnected and moving as one.

I must remember, however, that this is all just play, all just illusion. It only seems like all these stars, planets, people and other shapes exist separately and are doing all these interesting things. Actually they aren't. I am only playing them, in an imaginative game or play, in my mind. For a time, however, I actually began to think

I was these separate, individual humans. I forgot I was just playing. I got a little too wrapped up in the events and emotions that I had made up. I took them seriously. Making up the thinking-humans was interesting, but things gradually got too far out of balance. There was suspense, but work, effort, suffering and other forms of imbalance resulted. The play has become too real to Me. I made up too many rules and traditions; I became conditioned to actually thinking there were problems and found myself trying to solve them by the slow processs of thinking, forgetting they weren't real problems but ones I had made up. Often I felt I couldn't figure out a solution, or the one I did come up with was a mistake — with sometimes painful consequences. It was like having a nightmare.

I have pinched myself to wake up. I am trying to recover and get back to just playing, restoring balance in the cosmos of imaginary beings where I am at play, which means playing spontaneously and without purpose or goals as space Consciousness.

This is the ontological way of looking at earth life and human life. The secret of this way is to look at everything from the perspective of our self as pure Consciousness. It is the only real, true way to look at things. Looking at earth life and human life from the perspective of ourselves as humans is like actors in a play thinking that the play is real life. This is called "getting too wrapped up in the role." It is mixing up actual life with stage life. One is real, the other is imaginary.

This happened because as space Consciousness, playing out in our mind the roles of thinking-humans, we got too wrapped up in the drama, became conditioned to thinking and in the process momentarily forgot who we are. The result was our present amnesic half-life.

Who are you then? Who am I? As humans we are catalyst characters we've made up and are living through in our own mind. As humans we are several among the millions and millions of roles, shapes and forms we are playing out in our mind. As humans we are the same as pebbles, chips of wood, insects and drops of water. As humans, then, we are not in essence lords of creation. We are not important beings. We are nobodys. We are make-believe beings, parts we want to play, the way we'd pretend to be the cop in cops and robbers, or the master in the master and the slave — games we'd play as children outdoors. If we realize that, we won't get mixed up and take our roles, our titles, our positions, our financial or social status as humans, so seriously. The human roles are just pretense; just make-believe.

Our real identity is clear. In essence I am not so-and-so in this bag of skin. I am in essence pure Consciousness thinking all this up. You are too. Therefore we are the same. You (human) are another character we've dreamed up. You (human) are our (pure Consciousness') make-believe character. We are essentially the same. We are you and we are me. We are one and the same because we (you, I, humans) are all characters in our one same mind (pure Consciousness). Don't use your head to figure this out. Don't strain to understand. Just let it be. It will become clear.

The ultimate answer then to our question, "Who are we?" is:

We are the pure Consciousness of space, the creator of all dramas, the player of all plays. That is our real self. That is our identity. The who behind or underlying the human characters we feel more conscious of, is us, the one and only space Consciousness. There is an absolute unity between the self we act out in our bag of skin, and our self as space Consciousness.

What are we like? What is our nature?

We are eternal, infinite, pure, unembodied Consciousness. To the last, that is all there is in existence — pure Consciousness. All reality only appears to us to exist as various individual, separately existing shapes and forms such as humans and mountains, planets and suns. Actually, however, they exist only in our mind (as characters and events in a dream, or features such as the nose, ears, fingers and toes which appear to exist and are distinguishable, individual shapes but exist only as connected to our body).

Is there a God then?

Not a being existing off somewhere (or inside us) separately from us. That is dualism. There is in reality only one existing being — pure Consciousness. Dualism is a trap into which fall almost all the religions and groups trying to help us humans understand and cope with our situation. Even if they say this world is illusion, they cannot get away from efforts, programs and steps to unite with something or someone. There is no other to unite with; no steps necessary. Our Consciousness is all that really exists.

We are already what we want to be. We don't have to get to it or achieve it. All we have to do is wake up to the fact that we are it already. No steps necessary. No meditations, fastings, penances, classes or programs necessary.

We could say that if we are the One pure Consciousness then we are God. It would not be incorrect. We don't want to argue over words. But it is a problem for us that we are not awake, and we cannot help thinking of ourselves as humans right now. If we say we are God, so conditioned are we to think of God as something important, supreme, superior and supernatural, that we would then begin to imagine ourselves as even more superior as humans than we already imagine ourselves to be. It would not work for us to think of ourselves as God while immersed in human consciousness. If we were awake and thinking with space Consciousness we wouldn't make the mistake. But hardly any of us are thinking with space Consciousness yet. Most of us are asleep, wrapped up in our dreaming or playing the human game.

How did the world originate?

Essentially by being imagined as a world in our pure Consciousness. In reality it didn't originate as a physical, material existence. It originated in our mind, coming about through a process which we have had the fun of endeavoring to uncover in the games of science, study and research. Great fun. Games within games.

Was there a purpose?

No. It is just play — which is our nature, to eternally play, to daydream, to make up stories and the like — all in the eternal now. There was no purpose to the creation of this story and these characters, in the sense that there was something we were trying to bring out of it. That is cause and effect — an element in the human play. In space Consciousness we don't need anything. Within the play the humans have a purpose — of being catalysts — but not to serve God or anything like that. Their existence and activities are make-believe — not something serious.

Are earth and human life real?

In our Consciousness, yes. Out there, as separate, physical and material beings, no. Nothing exists like that. There never was anything, there never will be anything. Just pure Consciousness.

What are we seeing, hearing, feeling, tasting, and smelling then?

I've been talking about things as though they exist! Yes, they do exist, but only in our Consciousness. They seem very real to us playing in our human consciousness, but in space Consciousness we would realize they are only things we've thought up. We have created them in our imagination. So we should always remember that, never take them seriously, never get wrapped up in them, never think we can't do anything about them, never get overwhelmed when the play is troublesome, nor caught up in it when it's pleasant. The play can go on, working its way out, evolving as we've imagined, and we can have fun talking about it for ever and ever. We, however, must always remember that it's all in our head. It doesn't have any more reality than the images and happenings in a dream — like the characters and events in the dreams we have the humans dream. (Dreams within dreams, within dreams.)

What is going to happen to us humans and the earth in the play?

We have an infinite array of choices, all of which will eventually evolve and be played out in our Consciousness (Eventually of course is a human term. For us with our full Consciousness there is only eternal now. All the infinite eventualities are already there in the now of our mind). We are going to phase out the thinking-humans soon, though. They were catalysts to change things and set up for the next stage which is going to be even more interesting (to us humans that is. Interesting is a judgement — part of the catalyst play). In the next stage we will be playing beings with full Consciousnss and power. In the present thinking-human stage, we got too wrapped up in the play and our Consciousness became clouded. We are waking up to that, and arranging to recover full Consciousnss in all these characters.

Why then do I go on talking about what is going to happen to us and to the earth as though it were real?

If we remember everything is play, we can have fun discussing any or all of the ins and outs of earth life — what is going to happen to us and to the earth. The key is to remain consciously aware that we are talking about something that is play, make-believe, not real.

Neither you nor I therefore, must think that we are really so-and-so in a certain bag of skin, separate and disconnected from the continuum of space — which is the body of space Consciousness. The bag of skin, the name, the family connections, the activities — all are play. We only appear to be separate and on our own. When as humans our eyes are opened (or to put it in ontological terms our chakras are opened) we will see all the connections. You are connected to space Consciousness. I am connected to space Consciousness. So we are integral parts of the hologram of the universe.

We are recovering full Consciousness of this in the Earth Story. We will be playing new characters with full Consciousness. In the old characters, we will have to stop all the thinking and recover, or else simply phase ourselves quickly out of the play.

The way to recovery is the way of ontology. As humans, the way of ontology is a way of no thinking:

- to not think of ourselves as solid, physical, material beings;
- to not see ourselves as individuals, as separate existences;
- to not see ourselves as distinct from the space Consciousness body;
- to live spontaneously, according to our true, honest feelings;
- to realize that as humans we are mere characters given an imaginary life of our own in a game or play;
- to know that as humans we were originated in a mental drama by combining a form in nature with an ectoplasm from outside nature in a catalyst role that is coming to an end. So it is time to cut off and let go of catalyst life;
- to know our individual, solid, human body is enveloped and permeated by an energy body which in turn is enveloped and permeated by the infinite Consciousness Body or Space Body;

• to know that full Consciousness is in the space body, not in the energy body; and that complete connectedness to the space body and full Consciousness is our original state, a state that will characterize the future in the play of earth evolution;

• to know that in the play all is connected and moving as one — a living network;

• to live that way — live-net, aware that every thing is connected and moving as one in our mind;

• to know that in essence we are space Consciousness thinking up all this play in our own mind;

• to realize we are living space Consciousness, not so-and-so in a human bag of skin — and never to forget it!

Accessing Full Consciousness: The Way of No Thinking

Unlike the ways of philosophy or science in which we try to access knowledge through the processes of thinking, in the way of ontology we have to bypass the human mind. How? By not thinking.

In the play life we are acting out at present, the future will be new; it will be different. Children being born today are coming into this rapidly evolving world already naturally equipped to live in the coming age. Those of us who are adults will have to make some deep changes for us to be able to live in it. If we want to be part of it we'll have to respond to the impulse to let go of and shed our familiar catalyst past, and detach from all those things and values we cherish so deeply in our past role — family, schools, thinking, reading, manners, refinement, art, philosophy and religion, to name a few.

Being part of the coming age is simple in the sense of how little is required of anyone to do to be part of it; but that simple matter of switching our mind and giving up the old can be difficult. It's good to start following those voices or impulses that may be nudging us to become detached from our self-created drama, to be flexible, to let go, to go with the flow, to tune into the space around us for information instead of immediately turning into our mind or to a book, a guru or an expert. It will also serve us well to observe the youngsters carefully and learn from them. Adults who don't want to change, who want to clutch on to the old and familiar, will disappear (like the aristocracy at the time of the French Revolution). If we want to continue to live on, we have to find out more about the world of full Consciousness.

At the end of Chapter 15, I mentioned that what will replace money is information — not scientifically and technologically created and transmitted information, but cosmic Consciousness information — full Consciousness. How are we to access this information source? Not by following a guru in higher consciousness, finding a Yoga master, entering a Zen monastery, enrolling in a university program in consciousness, or consulting experts, visiting channellers, reading metaphysics books, or studying and thinking like mad. These were the ways to access information in the old catalyst days. If we use these methods, we are bound to reach only to our human mind which is limited and often erroneous.

How do we switch our minds from the old thinking patterns? Infants already have the knack of bypassing the usual thinking patterns we adults were guided into in the old catalyst period, thus giving them immediate access to space Consciousness. How do those of us who have been around so long, living in the algo-net world, doing our job well as catalysts, neutralize the strong conditioning we've been exposed to? We have to change to get it. Can we do that? And how do we do that?

The change is possible, but the strange thing about it is that we can't do anything positive about it on our own as humans. We can only let it happen, not block the change. We can stop doing those things which interfere with the autonomous processes going on in our space body. As catalyst humans we were used to setting out to conquer a challenge like this by some sort of effort, some program. It will be hard to resist that impulse to think we have to do something. It is simply a matter of waking up.

As humans we would set an alarm clock to wake us, or have someone come and call us or shake us. We are sometimes wakened by a noise. Otherwise we just wake up naturally. In the case of waking up to full consciousness how do we do it? Unlike the ways of philosophy or science in which we try to access some special knowledge through the processes of thinking, in the way of ontology we have to bypass the human mind. How? By not thinking. By just resonating. We open up our whole being to receive anything and everything by telepathy from our space Conscious-ness.

This means we do not process with our brain what comes in. We don't make judgments about anything: This is good, that is bad; I like this, I don't like that. Don't think. Don't take notes. Don't try to organize insights or inspirations logically. Don't try to find a formula in them. Don't try to control everything to go the way we (with a limited human viewpoint) want it to go. We don't make detailed plans anymore. We just let the flow of cosmic consciousness pass in and out of us freely. Only our real self, our space Consciousness Body/Mind enveloping and informing our human body/mind, can give us full Consciousness. What can we do? Just watch very trustfully and don't get in the way by thinking and falling back into catalyst thoughts and processes. After practice we find ourselves understanding very deeply and everything happening very nicely.

Where is this cosmic information coming from? It is not in the head of some old man with a beard in the sky. It is in the space body all around us. That is why I speak so often of accessing space Consciousness. Many people think they have done something great when they channel some spirit, or access some energy source through T'ai Chi, Chi Gong, or a meditational practice, or move some energy in Oriental medicine. That is nothing. It is reaching only the energy body. It can actually be very dangerous if you get some energy moving and don't know what to do with it. For example, if you don't know how to lead imbalanced energy (karma) out of your body, it gets trapped in you and can cause painful discomfort (sicknesses) and even death. What is more important, however, is that if you get wrapped up in playing with the energy body, you may stay there, satisfied. The only energy source that will do us any lasting good is our infinite Consciousness which is (in) the space body around us.

Why haven't we accessed it before? Because as catalysts, we weren't reared that way. For our catalyst role we were reared to use our heads, think with the human brain, and come up with the limited type of ideas the human brain could achieve. That was so that the limited achievements we labored to produce would pave the way for the next stage of evolution.

Now, our space Consciousness tells us that the job has been done. It is time to wind up our work or else as humans we will go too far. Now we are to stop thinking with our head and go directly to our space Consciousness around us for our knowledge and information. To do that we have to accustom ourselves to zero response. We return to zero. We have to die as it were. Not physically perhaps, but to all values and to all our familiar, conditioned responses such as thinking and planning. That is the same as death for most humans.

The nice thing about it all is that we don't have to worry about figuring out a comprehensive program to achieve this. We don't have to do penances and make sacrifices on our own. We don't need a new religion with doctrines, moral directives, rituals and prayers. We have only to learn to do nothing but open up and entrust ourselves to our surrounding space Consciousness. For the fact is, we can't do one blessed thing about it on our own human power.

Even in our make-believe human life, when we are sleeping we can't do anything about waking ourselves. We just wait until we wake up naturally. So too, as humans we can't do anything about waking up to full consciousness. It is only our space Consciousness enveloping us that can awaken us (whether our space Consciousness shakes us, gives us a wake up call, or sets an alarm off). We must not look upon recovering full Consciousness like we were getting a Ph.D. or becoming a saint. Those are typical algo-net approaches.

The only thing we can do is do nothing. Let Consciousness in our space body do the work. It knows best. As part of the live-net we just let go of the algo-net then wait for and respond to the wake-up impulses which we notice coming to us from our real self — our space Consciousness.

Our real self will know exactly what to do and when to do it. When our infinite space Consciousness wants to wake up, we will feel the impulse in our human consciousness. In fact, the wake up alarm may already have gone off. Do you feel drawn in new directions, perhaps at first for example to alter your food habits? As catalysts we've bought into the whole thing of modern eating and dining. Now we'll sense that changing. We've bought heavily into working and making a living. Algo-net catalyst hangers-on will still be trying to keep us firmly in the rut of consuming and contributing to the economy. They will be pressuring us into being involved. They will label us dropouts and counterculture freaks if we aren't wholeheartedly sympathetic to the methods and goals of the algo-net society. Yet, we will feel the pull to take it easy, to quit stressful jobs and do what we really want to do in life. We'll begin to discover contradictions and even foolishness in traditions, traditional values, causes, movements, set-ups and relationships we're so heavily into and worked up over. We can just say no to involvement in the usual catalyst mind-set and activities.

It will help to let our catalyst vocabulary become irrelevant from disuse and indifference: thinking, polls, research, planning, health, healing, sickness, doctors, hospitals, economy, making a living, job, work, education, school, learning, training, degrees, titles, immigration, visas, borders and national boundaries, possession, "that's mine!" laws, lawyers, courts, insurance, gambling, anger, fear, jealousy, war, peace and the environment. Decline to respect and kowtow to them any longer. Don't give them existence by thinking about them. When they come up say: "No thank you; there is a new way!"

Hesitating over or even forgoing the usual responses which we learned to pursue so enthusiastically in our catalyst past feels strange at first. Turning off our minds, letting go and resonating with our space Consciousness doesn't come easily. As we correspond more and more often to such impulses, however, we will find that accessing full Consciousnss will be painless and easy. No study. No sweat. No exams. No schools. No competition. No think tanks. No polls. No forums, seminars, conventions. You say they were fun? At times and for some catalysts. You want to continue on that way? Be my guest. If any of us do insist on continuing on, however, we will probably soon be eliminated by our real self. We will disappear. You think that kind of change will take centuries? The old stage is being phased out gradually, yes, but not over eons of time any more. The pace of change is picking up speed. It won't be long until the new era is firmly in place. We don't have much more time to enjoy thinking and arguing, figuring things out and problem solving.

However, I assure you, as frightful and impossible as this seems because of our catalyst conditioning, it will not be the end of the world. All of this, you'll find, can't compare with the state of full Awareness we will have and the kind of Life to which we are about to reawaken!

WHAT IS FULL
CONSCIOUSNESS LIKE?

*If we can go back upstream in the flow
of life to the point where we arrive at pure
space — nothingness — and can see that
state with our eyes, hear it with our ears,
feel it with our whole being, then we will
know a world in which there is no physical
or material phenomenon...where there is
nothing....where we are space itself. When
we can actually get that feeling we will
understand who or what we really are.
There is absolutely nothing there, so the feeling is like that of a fetus floating in the
womb. Just floating. We are the whole universe.*

Full Consciousness is the state of
being completely awake, fully aware of
the feelings or state of mind experienced
in the infinite timelessness, spaceless-

ness and nothingness of pure Consciousness.

I see in the hologram of life for the drama of our times — the end of the thinking-human stage — that we will be breaking ourselves from the spell of phenomenological thought, doing things without thinking, freeing ourselves from the trap of conditioned reliance on science and technology, accepting spontaneity, intuition, inspiration, telepathy, psychokinesis and teleporting, trusting the perfection of the universe and accessing our space Consciousness. We are going back into the safe and sane world of ontology.

I used to read about groups meeting to discuss ways to achieve higher consciousness. I was sure it would take some special talent, a special kind of person. It doesn't. All it involves is simply waking up — waking up to the fact that we are already such a being! As we become aware of it we will be convinced. We live very ordinarily in a world that we are hardly conscious of — cosmic space, which is a world of pure Consciousness. Although as humans we may not be conscious of it, the fact is that our enveloping and permeating Consciousness Body/Mind is guiding us. There is no need for thinking, since our space Consciousness is in charge. So relax.

Earlier we went back upstream in the flow of life to the point where we arrived at pure space — nothingness. If we can recapture that feeling, as though we can see that state with our eyes, hear it with our ears, feel it with our whole being, then we will know it: a world in which there is no physical or material phenomenon ... where there is nothing ... where we are space itself. When we can actually get that feeling we will understand who or what we really are. There is absolutely nothing there, so the feeling is like that of a fetus floating in the womb. Just floating. We are the whole universe of dreams. In this state we have a sense of perfect existence, of omnipresence, of complete extension ... the paradoxical state of thinking nothing but embodying every possible bud of thought. The enormous reaches of outer space, the celestial bodies, the uncountable marine species, the plants and animal kingdoms were born out of this creative Consciousness, each having this one same Consciousness. In that sense, the feeling is one of infinite thought, limitless, inexhaustible thought and yet no thought. Thinking limitlessly and yet not thinking. Doing nothing but doing everything. Making nothing but able to make up anything.

From the viewpoint of the world of phenomenology it looks like a Big Bang — all kinds of things coming out of nothing, and evolving in successive stages in a process of time. When we look at our own full Body, the Universe, however, we can even see things we will create in the future, even though there is absolutely nothing there. How? Because there is no time, no matter how much or where we search. There is no space either, so there is no distance between the point called Earth and the point called the Andromeda Nebula. The feeling is that of time-space synchronicity. It is the feeling of origin, of seeing simultaneously and doing simultaneously, occurring simultaneously, timewise and spacewise. This is the feeling of space you get when you go back upstream to where there is absolutely nothing.

There is no other way to express it other than to say it's like doing nothing but doing everything — both at the same time. Lao-tzu expressed it similarly: Doing nothing but enlightening. That is what the Tao is like. The Tao is space, the origin. Doing nothing but coming up with the whole phenomenal world — that is the work of space. That is the feeling of ontology. The only feeling that comes close to it is the feeling of the fetus, because it has no feeling of self or limit. It still retains its full space Consciousnss. It does not distinguish itself from its mother, or space, or the body. Therefore, we should all have this feeling of our origin deep within us. The awareness was there before we were born. It was there back upstream. It had to be because there wasn't anything else. Everything started from this state.

We, space, the Universe, aren't doing anything, so it would look like we can't do anything. Yet, we can do everything. Two opposites occurring simultaneously in space. In this state there is no desire, and so there is no unfulfilled desire. There is nothing lacking nor are there problems to be solved, from the start nor thereafter.

Naturally this constitutes a sense of total fulfillment, a third characteristic of full Consciousness. To the yogis of India, space Consciousness is much more of a joy than any cheap feeling of human happiness, human ability or human identity. For them, to recover awareness that our true identity is really space Consciousness, that we are after all pure space Consciousness imagining or dreaming ourself being and doing this and that, in this form and that form — that was true enlightenment! Still, they couldn't recover that full awareness of themselves as space Consciousness. Intellectually they posited such a state, but were unable to actually honestly feel it. The problem was that they tried — a sure giveaway that they considered themselves as separate, existing beings. Trying indicates a self-limitation. When you try you are in a vicious cycle because you are trying to so something in a world where trying isn't necessary and doesn't work. If we really realized we are space Consciousness playing various parts in our mind's imaginings, we wouldn't need to try to remember that we are space Consciousness.

Trying, in a world of no cause and effect, means we are trapped in cause-and effect-thinking — the make-believe catalyst world. Trying to do something not only involves a passage of time, but forms a cause to produce an effect. We are using cause-and-effect methods when what we really are is a being of a no-cause-or-effect world. It is self-contradictory and self-defeating from the start. This is why phenomenological ontology ends in a vicious cycle or an asymptotic line — a line that keeps on endlessly approaching another line or plane but is never able to break through to it.

This is the present state of humankind. Following phenomenological ontology we keep trying to make a jump back over into our original plane, but we just can't make it over the barrier. This state is close, but not ontology. In ontology there is no barrier. There is no jump or leap to make, because we already are what we want to be. All we have to do is stop thinking, stop trying, stop making up others, and just wake up!

As human beings we are convinced that we need to think in order to live, in order to work. If asked what was essential for us as humans to live and work, doubtlessly we would answer: thinking. To us it is the most important factor there is. We are sure that we couldn't do a thing if we didn't think — reason, imagine, investigate a cause, figure out a solution, determine ten steps to deal with whatever faces us. Of course, we say all of this without giving much thought to the matter. Well, let's just think about it then for a few moments.

When we take air into our lungs we do not need to think about what happens to it after that. Millions of things happen to it after that but we do not have to consciously make each of those millions of steps take place. They happen automatically — unconsciously, we say. When we put food into our mouth and swallow it, the process from then on is almost totally automatic — unconscious, we say. Ordinarily the troops on the front line of living action are operating totally outside our conscious awareness. Breathing, eating, digesting, producing energy, eliminating wastes, reproducing, sensing and even the processes of thinking are for the most part being carried on without our being conscious of what is going on.

So here we already have quite a few examples of some force, carrying us along, making us alive, without our being conscious of it. We know quite well that should we as humans offer to take over the whole matter ourselves and run all this with our thinking powers, everything would come to a screeching halt. We could never master all the intricate activities of switches turned on and off, quantities of this and that measured, adjustments made according to changing conditions. The power of thinking to accomplish anything for us is way back from the front lines, doing only menial tasks. The real front line work is being done by a force that is currently unconscious to us — space Consciousness — which ironically enough is not something or someone else, but us, our real self, pure Consciousness. It isn't us ectoplasm humans or our human thinking ability that is doing the real thinking which operates our minds and bodies.

All we need to do is give up our stubborn assumption that our thinking is what is doing everything for us, and that our thinking is necessary for everything to be done. Or, to put it the other way around, give up the stubborn resistance to the fact that what is making us, as humans, alive, moving us, making us operate as we are, putting thoughts into our heads, telling us what to do and where to go and when, is our real self, our space Consciousness — our cosmic autonomic nervous system. We can trust our full Consciousness. Then we can begin to find true inner strength. If we wake up and say, "I'm not just the little consciousness in this bag of skin but full Consciousness in the 'Body' of infinite space," we begin to recover omnipotence. Free will, suffering and evil, choices, actions and events, other peoples' talents and successes, other peoples' opinions of us, mistakes, our houses, cars, people, countries, scenery, all of which seem so realistic, are infinitely well-made-up images, shapes and forms, dreams and plays. There is nothing out there. The only thing that exists is our pure infinite Consciousness playing away without end in our infinite unembodied mind.

We have decided, however, in our space Consciousness, that in the drama of human life, the human will have trouble accepting a lot of things, even though they become obvious upon a bit of reflection. Take the classic problem: What is the now? We are conscious of what the future is. We can say that ten seconds from now is still the future. At what point, however, does it become past? As you count down to one second what happens? It passes and immediately becomes past. What happend to now? Split the last second into tenths of a second, hundredths of a second, millionths of a second, billionths of a second. No matter how infinitely you divide that last second, it is either still future, or — zzzzip! — it has become past. To our minds, "now" is a nothing moment. It is a moment of which we have no consciousness. We have an idea of what a second is, and perhaps what a tenth of a second is. Beyond that, however, our human consciousness becomes less and less capable of grasping the reality.

Well, we better look a little closer at this idea of doing without thinking. We've seen it is true that for humans as well as for plants and animals, the front line of action is being handled by a force that carries on without the need of the humans' or animals' thinking. For humans, thinking follows soon afterward, whereas for plants and animals, thinking comes out only here and there at points such as when they are attacked by an enemy, or when they look for the opposite sex, or feel like eating and looking for food. The rest is almost completely automatic — autonomous. They carry on automatically with synergy. They move in response to vibrations — by resonance. Resonant relationships are much more accurate than thought relationships. It is only humans who boast that thought is the most accurate and wise way in the universe. No other animals we know of in the universe share that conviction. It would seem better for us not to have that feeling, but we dreamed it up that way so that in humans we would act as catalysts. Animals live and move according to instinct, in accord with the impulses of cosmic consciousness.

It is only on the earth stage where we thought up the play calling for us human beings to push thought up to the front lines and expect it to do the major work. All we have to do is to relieve our human mind of the tremendous burden of operating everything on its own and let it rest in the cosmic flow of omniscience — full Consciousness, an automatically operating flow of functions and chain reactions. With full Consciousness, instead of always jumping in to do something or solve something with thought, we make use of the autonomously operating powers of our infinite Consciousness. Full Consciousness can and does do everything. That's what it's like.

SURPRISE! THERE ARE NO OTHERS

OUR IDENTITY AS COSMIC ONLY CHILD

We are not separate beings, but firmly and tightly One with our Space Body. With that consciousness we are liberated from the anxiety and insecurity that drive us as catalyst humans to pursue individual ownership, private property, wealth, and power. It is in connectedness and oneness that we are completely rich, completely powerful, completely secure, completely whole.

A major block to full Consciousness is the feeling of separateness. We have seen how true life flows out of a living network in which everything is tightly connected together, moving as one. However, during the catalyst phase of the Earth Story, we humans operated under the illusion that we were distinct, individual, solid body beings. In America we see individualism developed to its extreme limits. It was a clever stratagem of the ectoplasms and it worked beautifully. In fact, we are witnessing its spread around the world. The illusion served well to attract us humans into the kind of lifestyle that would change the earth for the next stage of evolution.

The strengths of this mind-set in promoting catalyst activity were obvious. From here on in, however, it will be a block and a burden to full Consciousness. Full Consciousness is much more satisfying and powerful than private ownership, individual human rights, and separateness. Yet, we are still convinced that separateness is our nature, that we are distinct, individual solid bodies moving around on our own.

For us humans, part of the problem is the fact that it was in the play for us to rely on senses for our knowledge. With eyes we believe we have ultimate access to reality. We cherish our eyesight. In the big picture of things, however, our physical vision severely limits our consciousness. When we look at our skin, for example, we are sure that it is a solid surface. Or when we look at each other walking around, we are sure that we move and operate on our own power, as though we have a hundred-year battery inside, or some other sort of internal energy source in us enabling us to move around and be completely self-sufficient.

Through the use of instruments such as microscopes we now know that the surface of our skin is composed of cells between which there is quite a bit of space. In fact, with the use of high power, high magnification computer instruments, we can get down to the same level of their size — to nano space. At that level the impression is much the same as we have at our own human level of operation. Each of the cells, molecules, atoms and particles have a unique, distinguishable shape and function. They look like they are all operating on their own, completely distinct from and completely unconnected to one another, with gaps of space between them. Yet, when we return to our human level of vision, the perspective of distance enables us to perceive that they are indeed connected and all moving as one inside our body, and that they couldn't exist except by reason of that connection. Relative to each other they appear separate, but in reality they are connected together and moving as one. In other words, we are all bodies within bodies, within bodies.

So we should be able to understand the possibility that though we humans look disconnected and alone, separate and individual in our operation, we are, from a larger perspective, connected and moving as one inside larger and larger bodies enveloping us. There is no instrument to enable us to see the connections. Only full Consciousness provides that perspective and enables us to see our Oneness.

If we can have an open mind for an instant, we can look honestly at our situation and accept the fact that instead of our individualism being an unmitigated blessing, this perception of separateness is at the root of our feelings of uneasiness, fear, anxiety, competition, distrust, jealousy and envy, revenge, violence, alienation, loneliness and despair.

Most of our philosophies and religions, however, have attributed the situation to some mistake we humans made and the evil behavior we continue to display. Their conclusion has always been that we humans were some sort of defective product of the universe.

Schopenhauer was a good example of this. He was quite distressed by the thought of human imperfection. Being European he thought in humanist terms, but upon coming in touch with the Indian philosophy that all things are Brahman (God) he got mixed up. Why am I here? Why do I exist here thinking this? If there is only one reality, God, or the Universe, then why am I, God, feeling ignorant? Why do I want to learn things? Philosophy is an inquiry into things, and to inquire into things means that I am trying to know because I don't know. If I am really God, omniscient and omnipotent, I don't have to inquire into anything. I would only try to learn if I were ignorant. That is why people become philosophers.

First of all, Schopenhauer obviously could not accept the theory of Oneness proferred by the Yoga philosophy. Secondly, the fact that humans become scientists and philosophers illustrated to him the defectiveness of human intellect — in other words, that humankind is a defective product of the Universe. It depressed Schopenhauer no end to think that he was a defective product. He couldn't conceive of God making anything that was not perfect and he wasn't prepared to consider the possibility that God was momentarily confused. Yet, it looked to him as though that is what had happened: The Universe, Brahman, Who was omniscient and omnipotent, made the heavenly bodies, plants and animals so magnificently and then somehow failed when making the human! Schopenhauer's philosophy was, therefore, very pessimistic.

Of course, he was missing the key. He no doubt shared some part of the mentality of his times that the physical, material world actually existed on its own, separate from God, and that there was a real problem of good and evil, a problem that hounded humans through the centuries despite the fact that some religions, those following the Bible, for example, placed the blame squarely on the humans. This explanation employed the metaphor of a test we were put to at the time of our origin — choosing to accept living happily within the given, paternally provided garden of Eden, eating from the tree of life; or choosing to strike out on our own to see if we couldn't improve on our situation by seeking knowledge of our own on the tree of knowledge of good an evil, instead of just having it.

Neither Schopenhauer nor any others at the time or since, realized that the human was only a characater in the mental play of God. God did not fail in making the human. In the first place, the earth and humans were only made up in the infinite Imagination; and secondly, in the drama, the ectoplasm human was a fully effective actor to do the job of catalyst. We have already established this, but since we were catalysts for so long we are deeply conditioned to the catalyst mentality of our being separate, distinct individuals.

Here it will help us to consider how it happened in the play that we came to feel so much on our own, so distinct and separated from everything else around us, so that we can once again recognize the solution that lies immediately before us. It is important to make note before we go on, however, that in this matter we are up against the greatest of paradoxes: how we humans could be defective if we were made by a God who is perfect; how we humans could be defective if we are God; how existence can be such an absolute unity when it looks like we have such separateness; how everything can be in an eternal now, when we talk about history, evolution and other consecutive events.

The problem is multiplied by our language which is understandably based on our experience in the physical, material world. We have no terms or concepts for any existence outside of the world we experience with our senses, even if we've had extrasensory experiences. More specifically, words can't come close to describing what it was like for us as space Consciousness to come to the feeling of separateness, because there is no progression of events in pure Consciousness; everything is in eternal now. Yet when as humans we try to talk about the play, we are thrown back on terms of space and time. We have to describe it as a process taking place in successive events, in past tense. However, if we don't get locked into the human thought content of the words and let them convey other meanings above and beyond that, as we know they can, then we can get some inkling of the problem. Even though the explanation will not be satisfactory to our human mind, it can be helpful in orienting our consciousness. We must leave it to our real self and intuition to grasp the reality.

How did it happen that we came to be conscious of separateness?

The answer is in our nature as space Consciousness. As humans we think of our space Consciousness as an infinitely fertile imagination coming up with all sorts of ideas, stories and worlds. When as space Consciousness we made up the Earth Story, our consciousness went out in waves, which formed a flow and the waves began to cross each other, creating eddies of whirling energy. These whirling eddies produced interference patterns, the appearance of various shapes and forms. One might say cosmic illusions. (We know how atoms which are mostly space and therefore simply centers of whirling energy, give rise to the appearance of varying shapes and forms such as organs, muscles, skin, rocks, wood, steel and air.)

Physicists and other scientists talk of substances in addition to space in the universe and they speak as though there were actual motion connnected with these substances. Since we as space Consciousness are everything, tightly packed, we can produce no motion in substance. We can produce motion only in illusion. There is no real motion accompanying any substance, and that goes for the black holes as well. There is only the illusion of motion.

Because nothing comes from nothing, it is clear that these motions of images, plays and stories had to come out in perfectly symmetrical pairs according to a formula: $+ - = 0$ — i.e. nothing. Noting that both plus and minus sides came out, we maintained awareness that the perfect balance (nothingness/infinity) was retained. The motion was then a whole, a complete pair. When we were making up the Earth Story, everything went smoothly as long as we took everything for what it was — nothing. All we felt was a sense of play. This was the state of cosmic homeostasis.

Though it could never happen that both sides would not come out in balance, consider the possibility that we, space Consciousness, became absorbed in only the plus or minus of something. The ancients called that a karma motion — one that is only half-perceived, depriving us of the whole picture and interfering with our detachment and perfect balance. Getting so wrapped up, we found play taking on an air of seriousness. Not having the whole picture, we began to make up something that wasn't really there.

Picture several children going outside to play. They go out to have fun. You hear them shouting and giggling. I'll be king and you be the slave. They play happily. They are aware that they are just playing. It's not real life to be taken so seriously. They have the healthy feelings of everything being fine and lots of fun. Suddenly one of them starts to get overly concerned about one side of the play: "You are always the king. I don't like being the slave. I want to be the king!" The child loses sight of the whole picture. The play has become too real. The child is beginning to take it too seriously. They begin to argue. Mother hears them fighting and says, "All right, that's enough. If you're going to fight, you're coming inside."

This is a metaphor for what happened to us as space Consciousnss. Symmetry was the key! This enabled us as space Consciousnes to produce apparent shapes and forms in our mind and yet retain consciousness that there was nothing to get overly excited about. Every time we made a plus, we made a minus also. Together they cancelled each other out and maintained the even, balanced consciousness of play. Nothing real was happening. It was just play. Symmetry, or keeping things in proper perspective, was the key to play.

Physicists are unsure about symmetry. They used to think that the universe made things in perfect symmetry. They are wondering, however, about a break of symmetry in the world of elementary particles: Are there perhaps cases of non-symmetry? Ultimately, never. If we add up everything in the universe, the particles and anti-particles will add up to zero. Add up particles rotating clockwise and those rotating counterclockwise and the answer is again zero. Add plus-charged particles and minus-charged particles; we get $+ - = 0$. Therefore, no matter where or how far we look in the universe, the state of nothingness continues.

Imagine the surface of the sea, perfectly still. If there were absolutely no waves or flows on earth, all the seas of the earth would be dead calm, like mirrors. Consider this state of the sea as the beginning state of the universe in the Earth Story. Now try to make waves there. Watch and see how they are made. You can let the wind blow or anything you like. Because of the relationship of action and reaction, the only way you can make a wave that rises up is to make another, dipping down next to it — a plus and a minus. Action and reaction cause the number of protrusions above the surface (crests) to be the same as those dipping below the surface (troughs). Adjoining waves may not look exactly symmetrical, but if you add them, the total amount of wave above and below the surface is exactly equal. You can say it in the formula: $+- = 0$. It holds for waves and for every blessed thing in the universe. Motion can only be produced by symmetry. Symmetry is a law of motion: action and reaction. Newton discovered this. It is the way that we as pure Consciousnes dreamed up the universe in the Earth Story.

Keeping track of symmetry, keeping the whole picture, was essential. As long as we, space Consciousness, did not become overly absorbed in one activity, our play would have been unbounded and free. However, the fact is this did not happen. When we created the solar system, the human being and the human drama, we focused attention on only one side of the plus/minus equation. We lost balance there, which in turn means that we lost our sense of freedom and became absorbed in our own drama. We lost awareness of the fact that as humans we were merely an illusion in our larger space Consciousness imagination. More importantly, we forgot that we are space Consiousness, omnipotent and omniscient, in the larger context called the universe.

As space Consciousness, we should realize that we alone exist and everything else is just an imaginary character we are thinking up in our mind for play. We should not feel bothered by others, since there are no others nor for that reason should we feel in any way bound by any laws. The fact is, however, as humans we have come to think of ourselves as bound by biological, physical and chemical laws, and that nothing can be done about them. The environment surrounding us also works according to laws — natural and social laws — and so it is not free. In short, the feeling of being totally free, omniscient and omnipotent, and the memory of having created all the phenomena in the universe have evaporated from our Consciousness.

We went on in that state, even though it meant experiencing what it was like to have only limited consciousness, having to learn, make mistakes, even suffer. The human, the individual and humankind are nothing but us, pure Consciousnss, in that self-created state of imbalanced consciousness, bound into what we called time, space and separateness. our mind was filled and burdened with imbalance.

If we had quickly recovered by balancing our appraisal of those particular whirlpools and seeing the whole picture again, the fun would not have gone out of our play. Like the children, however, the longer we invested in our drama, the more absorbed we got. All our infinitely expanded attention and consciousness was pulled into the narrow confines of those shapes within the physical world and drama, especially the human drama.

Now, as space Consciousness, we are waking up to that and want to recover our original state of awareness and play. How are we to recover, to free our full Consciousness and power while playing in this physical universe? How can we reverse the centuries of conditioning that have ingrained in us this habit of viewing ourself as separate individuals, a habit that is so deeply etched in the whole chain of evolution down to the particles?

Since we want the catalyst work to be phased out, we are first of all beginning to make up new beings without that old individualist mind-set. Then we will change those already made up characters in whom we want to continue on into the next era. We are reprogramming the responses of these existing humans so that they do not get all wrapped up in the drama. We are giving them an impulse to look at the whole picture, to presume there is another side to everyone and to everything and look for it, and to remember we are all connected and move as One.

As space Consciousness, We will relieve ourselves of that burdensome mind-set of separateness and individualism. We will foster a realization that remaining in the catalyst mind-set, looking at separateness and individualism as a value to cling to and preserve, is a burden and a weakness, whereas, letting go of individualism and separateness and recovering awareness of the connectedness of all things brings profound relief and strength. Yet, how will we eliminate and reverse the strong conditioning? How will we set ourselves and our world free?

If we remember that in the Earth Story we are just playing, we will be able to recover memory of ourself as space Consciousness. At the same time, we will regain perspective that as humans we are not separate and cut off, but firmly and tightly one with our space Body since we exist only in our space mind. We will know the feeling of complete well-being that pure Consciousness enjoys. Even though we, pure Consciousness, exist solitary, alone in infinite space, we will know that having the most fantastic lover and the most fulfilling relationship possible as humans is nothing in comparison to this cosmic well-being.

We will be liberated from the anxiety and insecurity that drive us as catalyst humans to pursue individual ownership, private property, wealth, power and happiness — values which only accentuate separateness, destroy relationships and create fear and sadness. We will be freed from the unhappiness and despair described by many of the modern philosophers. It is in connectedness and oneness that we are completely rich, completely powerful, completely secure, completely whole. That is our original state: pure, infinite, unembodied Consciousness.

CORRECTING THE COSMIC HOLOGRAM

Trying to fix life here by environmental movements, health movements, peace movements and the like; opening chakras by endless, complicated human practices; efforts to control human thought; penances; rituals; prayers; sacrifices; and other human goings on — all are equally just that: human catalyst gestures in a play. Making a comeback depends on our awakening to the fact that we are space Consciousness and on our dying to everything human.

We are in fact space Consciousness. We as humans are creations of our own play. Although we are space Consciousness, we have become absorbed in this illusion called the human drama as though it were reality. Yet, in real reality there is only one existing being — our Consciousness. So, the question is how can we evolve a new illusion that achieves the plus/minus balance (nothingness) which is the essence of the cosmos?

Whether we view ourselves as humans or ourself as space Consciousness makes a difference, because the way we recover as space Consciousness varies from the way we have the humans in our play recover from their problems. We have had the ectoplasms guide the catalyst humans to meditate, fast, do penance, try to be enlightened and recover union with a God or the universe in an effort to solve their problems. Doing any or all of these things as humans, however, accomplishes nothing toward recovering from the problem we have. As space Consciousness, we recover in a different way.

To recover from the false image we're laboring under in our mind, we have to dispell the imbalance by focusing on the whole picture again. Imagine how difficult this is, however. We (you, I) are pure Consciousness so habituated to a world of slow, imperfect thinking and to such a mind-boggling array of relationships, traditions and rules that we cannot easily just shake our heads and throw off the mind-set. No matter what we start out to do now, we have this deeply ingrained habit of thinking or feeling that there are things we have to do. Though we know we are space Consciousness and only have to want this or that and it is done, (after all, it's only in our mind) we don't have that confidence. We can easily walk on water, but we hesitate because we haven't been doing it for some time. We know that we can create reality with our thoughts, but our thoughts are earth-bound, human bound.

We humans can relate to the fact that when we dream or daydream, fantasize or make up some story in our heads, the characters and events, no matter how realistic they at times appear, are not objective, solid objects running around in our heads. They are simply mental forms. The image or daydream can be very simple or complicated. It can be pleasant or a nightmare. When we realize we are dreaming or daydreaming, we simply take it as a dream or a fantasy. In fact, we can follow it with interest. But if we happen to lose track of the fact that we are dreaming or fantasizing, and feel for a time that the images in our minds are real, then we can get pretty wrapped up in the story, sometimes having a pleasant time, but other times getting quite upset, angry and afraid.

If we can fully awaken to the reality of the universe, we can remember that it was we who created all this in our mind, that we are still making it up in our mind, and thus recover equilibrium. We are still too wrapped up in the Earth Story, however, to think with clarity. The part of us that has lost this full Consciousness and is now stumbling around in partial consciousness is ourself as human.

We have to remember that there are no suns, planets, marine life, vegetation, animals or humans existing separately from us, pure Consciousness, any more than there is sometimes a fantastic or disgusting person at home, school or work. Such images are not reality but false pictures we've made up in our mind by focusing on only one side or the other of the whole. The only existing reality is us, pure Consciousness. Humans and all these other forms are characters and props in a dream or drama going on eternally, without end, in our mind. The idea that humans are separate, substantive, objective realities constructed out of nothing by a God is the trap of dualism.

As humans we lost the sensation of cosmic omni-science and omnipotence, and instead learned to rely, unbelievably, on science and technology as a replace-ment to fill the gap. Science and technology are substitutes we have turned to during this period when we find ourselves to have forgotten the knack of cosmic omniscience and omnipotence. After all, how-ever, science and tehnology are ultimately the workings of our space Consciousness mind, not our human mind. They reflect our position, of course — unwilling to see things from all sides in full perspec-tive. Choosing momentarily to not draw on our full powers, we struggle along with only science and tech-nology. When we reestablish contact with the fact that we are space Consciousness, science and technology will disappear. Religion will too, and of course politics, economy and culture. This will be taking place in the twenty-first century.

How are we going to reawaken to the fact that we are space Consciousness that quickly? We have become conditioned to think of ourselves as so-and-so in a certain bag of skin, of a certain gender, a certain country, a certain race, a creature of planet earth, of the Milky Way galaxy. What we have lost sight of as we have gone on playing this infinite mental video game of waves, eddies and whirlpools is that as humans we are still the Universe itself, life itself. We are the actor, *par excellence*, playing out billions and billions of parts. In this bag of skin we are only one character. This being the case, the way to regain our cosmic memory is to walk off the stage for a bit, take a breather and remember we're each just playing a part. All we have to do is come to our senses and realize this drama here is all a play. Go back upstream and find that our human body and mind are only phenomena produced like a whirlpool, or holographic image, in one corner of the universe. Accept that the play got mixed up in parts and confusion ensued. Resist the attractions of the illusion that we are basically a separate, individual, solid-body human being. Recover the realization that we are the Universe, pure Consciousness, thinking up and operating ourself as a human or any other number of forms. We will remember that we can remain human, living out the drama of life on an earth, and at the same time maintain our cosmic identity — literally a cosmic being.

Sounds simple, but it isn't easy. The problem goes way back. This imbalance very clearly occurred at the stage when we were dreaming up the sun — or should I say twirling out the thought waves that resulted in those whirlpools of energy or interference patterns which created the appearance we today call the sun. It was at that root point that we lost track of the symmetry in the horizontal and vertical coordination of eddies in our thought waves (appearance only). It appeared to us that, in composing the whirlpools we call matter, the balance was off. So at that point we could no longer just watch effortlessly as the formations went on taking place.

That was the first thinking. It was a hitherto completely foreign feeling — being bound by laws, having to make effort. As sun we were now a being that had become unable to carry on our play of creating more eddies without all this preoccupation. We no longer created easily and automatically. From within ourself as sun we produced more crossing waves and hence new eddies — planets. We were experiencing difficulty, however. In planet earth we were much worse off. We had come forth out of the sun as a huge being of living rock. In that being we went on producing more eddies — this time molecules and cells. We were very self-conscious of being bound by laws.

Today, as humans we don't think of the nebulous gases, the galaxies, the sun, or the planets as living beings capable of creating anything, thanks to the pronouncements of science. The fact is, however, that in the story, everything is living to some degree.

(I say in the story because, don't forget, in reality humans, suns, planets, earth, trees, rocks, cars and houses exist only as our images. We, as pure infinite Consciousness, exist. That's it. Everything else is illusion.)

As Earth, we continued to dream on. our thought waves flowed, crossed and eddied until the whirling energies produced the appearances of bacteria, plants and animals. As successive layers developed further, that appearance of thinking, the subsequent loss of memory about everything being connected, and the false image of others we had made up in our mind, an image with no basis in reality, took on the force of almost unchangeable habit by the time it had progressed as far as the human.

Supposing there were a sun somewhere in the universe that had not been formed by whirling eddies slightly out of symmetry? What would it be like? It would be a straight thinking, straight doing sun. Then there would be straight thinking, straight doing planets. Straight thinking, straight doing plants, animals and humans would also be possible. Perhaps there is such a world somewhere. Buddha must have thought so, because he spoke of such a land. At any rate, we as Universe would be operating it all with complete Consciousness. Without ever forgetting what we were doing, we would be playing the parts of celestial bodies, plants, animals and humans. In none of these would there be any sense of competition or struggle, nor any sense of helping out others either. All would be operating with synergy, autonomously, within our one Body.

Because each form in that scenario would be us as Universe very clearly playing a part, the sense of existence and identity would be completely different than it is in this Earth Story in which we are now operating (in our mind). Here, our sense of existence and identity has become warped. We've actually forgotten for all practical purposes Who we really are. We've come to think we're just a human, whereas being human is just a part we made up. We wanted to make changes on the earth that would lead naturally toward the next stage of the play.

To do that we could have given new directions to the ectoplasm leading the human. Make it clear that the work of catalyst has been successfully completed and so now full Consciousness is going to be restored to ourself acting as humans. Since the problem began as far back as the asymmetrical earth sun, however, we have decided to go to the root of the problem and restore the sun to full Consciousness. We, as space Consciousness, want to redo the whole thing.

To redo the whole thing, we have to start from the level of ultimate root particles and elementary particles, of course. Unless we correct their condition, we will not be able to straighten out our act as humans. To overcome the habits that have become ingrained in our space Consciousness, we will have to work our way back out of them, vertically and horizontally, in order and with coordination, down into the organs, tissues, cells, molecules, atoms, elementary particles and to the ultimate root particles of the human forms.

Can we, however, have the humans fly to the sun and fix it, or to the planets, or inside the Earth and fix them? Hardly. Then how about starting with metals and materials like ceramics which we humans made out of minerals around us? How about fixing them from their very root so that they are in perfect plumb, with perfect coordinates horizontally and vertically? Not very easy either. When it comes down to concrete steps to take, what should we do to restore this dream? If we try to reorganize present-day science and technology, we face a limit in principles. Since the systems of laws governing our solar system are unique to this part of the cosmos, we cannot consider these laws universal.

There is, however, something very close at hand in which this re-doing can be accomplished — the human being. The most elementary particles of nebulous gas, of the sun, the planets, mantle, magma, rocks, bacteria, plants and animals — all these stages are collected, unified and embodied in the human. They are all holographically present in the human.

As part of the evolutionary continuum of nature, the human body is more complete than any of the minerals in the body. A mineral has stopped there, but a human body has passed through the mineral stage, and so it extends further out in the continuum than even the sun because it has everything of all the prior stages of evolution in it. It is a composite of everything within our solar system. The human body is the best sample we have of the cosmic continuum, with layers and layers of dimensions. The human body is a multidimensional computer, a multidimensional cosmic timer, a multidimensional cosmic compass, a multidimensional cosmic engine and a multidimensional cosmic machine. There is no other cosmic machine as complex and organic as the human body.

So, all we have to do to re-do everything from the start is to remake the human.

The first to grasp this was Yoga. Intuitively the yogis had the idea of points in the human body where cosmic energy should flow freely in and out. They called these points chakras. They figured these chakras must be clogged or closed for some reason, so they devised hundreds of practices with a view to opening the chakras and thus giving the human freer access to Brahman's energy. Obstacles or impurities are aberrations. So if there is impurity between cells, remove the impurity, then the body's power can be returned to its original, balanced state and it will feel rejuvenated. If there is any aberration between minuscule organs composing the cells or any impurity between still smaller molecules, the cosmic power of the cells can be restored if the aberration or impurity is removed. There are deviations inside the atoms which make up the cells and within various elementary particles inside the atoms. If they are corrected it is possible for the particles and atoms to have cosmic, ultra-super power.

What would happen, the yogis thought, if all the chakras were opened and all impurities, deviations and blocks were removed from us? We would experience Superlife. None of them ever attained this stage, however. There were too many steps, too many practices; and they were doing it as humans. Like those in all other programs, disciplines and religions, they couldn't get away from the dualism that was part of the catalyst mind-set. (No reflection on them, mind you; we just didn't intend to attain Superlife in them yet.)

There is a way, however, and it's meant to be discovered now. Not too many years ago, we gave our human self a clue. Since the time of catalyst work was nearing an end, we revealed something we'd dreamed up long before but kept hidden during those catalyst

ages — the hologram. In the dream play, we constructed this present physical world like a multidimensional
hologram. There is a very unique feature to a hologram. If you take any piece out of a hologram, and look
at it, you can see the entire hologram; whereas, if you
take one piece out of a photograph and look at it you
only see that part of the picture you took out.

So, we had it in our mind that if we would change
a few little pieces of the Universe hologram called
humans, we could change the entire hologram.
Awaken a few humans, then! That would be a quick
way for us to bring about full recovery of the whole
universe. That is what we are in the process of doing
now. That will bring a new stage of earth life. We want
to recover soon, so that the catalyst action we instituted
doesn't go too far, the earth ceasing to exist, for example, in which case we would lose our opportunity as
space Consciousness humans to restore the balance of
the Universe.

By the twenty-first century a new play will be
doing dress rehearsals and the old play will bow off the
stage. Changing a few pieces of the hologram called
humans is the way we have decided to bring the
change about. The nature of this change is to restore
cosmic equilibrium through regaining the memory of
who we human beings really are. We are integral parts
of One Universe, and the Universe is a bunch of forms
appearing to be created by the eddying of thought

waves in our mind — space Consciousness. No dualism possible — only Oneness.

We will be able to balance our mind-set in every dimension within the hologram, back through all the stages of evolution — from human bodies back through organs, tissues and cells, back through molecules, atoms and particles, back through the planet to the sun. The entire cosmic evolution of the solar system will be rebalanced in an orderly way inside the human body. We will become again a fully living network — a cosmic organism or being. Cosmic homeostasis will be restored.

In the coming age when we regain the memory of being space Consciousness, and recover the state we were in before, what will it be like? There will be no sense of separation between us and others and our environment. There will be no sensation of being bound by various laws inside our body. We will be able to rid our self of impurities, rearrange any blocks that are out of plumb, and restore balance wherever needed.

What will life in the twenty-first century be like? This is a topic of great interest to humans as this millenium draws to a close. Predictions are rife. Most of them, however, simply presume a continuation of life on the same level of human civilization where we've been for centuries. We've seen that this is not to be the case.

The simplest stage direction possible for the new play "Twenty-first Century, Live-Net Life" is going to be:

- to rearrange the various elements or options with-in the human into a cosmic machine or cosmic organism;
- and then project the substance inside the new body outward, to make organic living materials (beings) that are on a level unknown to this world before.

Then, instead of producing lifeless ceramics as we humans do now, we as the new universians or cosmo-beings will be able to make softer, more pliable, living bodies. We'll be making organic (living) metals, organic ceramics, organic plastics that will be like tissues we now see in living bodies. These will flow out of us, as will also organic, living machines. If all the chakras open, the brain of this new universian will no longer be the human brain it is now, but a cosmic brain. If all the chakras open, the cell nucleus (which now is the brain for the cell) will no longer be the cell nucleus it is now, but a new kind of being. If the new brain and the new cell nucleus and the new atom nucleus are collected on a line extending outside of us, they will form an organic, living computer — not a regular computer, but a cosmic computer. Sort of a cosmic electronic brain.

The present-day media for producing the forms of life as we know it are we humans and our creations — science, technology and systems (civilization). The media for producing the forms of life in the twenty-first century will be the new universians or cosmo-beings. No other order will be thinkable from now on. Nothing will appear on the line extending out from present-day media — humans and the creations of humans. As we recover the Consciousness of our cosmic dimensions, an infinite number of things will become possible. The horizon is limitless. Being confined in human life as we know it today is like being an insect in a bottle or container. Our world is very narrow. If we could get out of the container for a moment, we would see the vast space all around us and the inconceivable number of phenomena there are. We would see, hear and feel how insignificant our ideas are for new breakthroughs tomorrow. Outside of the confining container of humanness is infinite possibility and play — intuitive, cosmic play, cosmic game-playing, cosmic drama.

From ancient times people have thought that humans could become happy as they are, as humans or individual beings. This however, was an illusion after all. No one has ever become endlessly happy as an individual human being. Fortunately we will not remain individuals, little pieces of a hologram. Will we achieve that when we get to heaven or find union with God? Not if by that you imply that heaven and God are separate from us. When we awaken to the fact that instead of being humans or earthlings we are universians, we will have that indescribable realization that we are the thinker-upper of the entire universe. The people we look at now are not others. They are mirror image reflections of our own self, floating in our infinite Space Body/Mind. Since we are mutually the whole universe, we can and should truly say: I am you, you are me. We have a holographic relationship. We are holographic beings and our dealings with each other are no longer individual-based. All us phenomena in the universe overlap. That is natural because we are all characters and props in a dream or play we are playing in our Consciousness. Everything overlaps.

We will not be flinching then like we do now. There won't be any more feelings like: "I'm falling behind others." "Others are richer than me." Or, "I don't want to be poorer than others," or "I want to be prettier than others," or, "They are more important than I am," or "Nobody loves me." There are no others. This is the Consciousness we will have in the coming century. We (you, I) will feel that everything is inside our own Space Body/Mind. Everything is in us and we can make any phenomenon in the universe now with time-space synchronicity. This Consciousness is the base for the organic, living society that is to come, for the cosmic civilization that will dawn.

What this Consciousness is like is not a mystery. We have a sample of it, right here in our human body. The human body is only an imperfect cosmic continuum, and yet the eyeballs and navel do not have any feeling that they are completely separate individuals. They are simply one with the complete body and spirit.

Nevertheless, we will see many beings without this Consciousness failing to make the transition back into this organic, living society. Many humans and many beings created by human consciousness will not identify with this state of affairs. We will witness the disappearance of many companies, organizations, governments and civilizations once supposedly great and powerful but lacking this Consciousness.

If we look carefully inside our mind or in our dream now, we realize there are parts or characters in which we have become carried away. We've forgotten that they are simply us playing a role. There are parts of our Body that are holding out, saying, "I'm me. I'm not just a part of some bigger 'body.' I'm a separate, unique creation." This is simply karma. It is a way of thinking that has become an unconscious habit during the long process of being passed on to us in generation after generation of cosmic whirlpool spread.

Still, we as space Consciousness want to regain cosmic Consciousness in certain humans. We want to recover awareness that none of the myriads of beings in the universe are separate individuals but all one in us, the one Body/Mind of the Universe. We will see holographically that the parts *are* the whole. We will see the hologram moving on its own without any distinction between the parts and the whole, which means without any contradictions or inconsistencies, without inequalities, without mysteries. We will understand that good and evil, happiness and unhappiness, richness and poverty, war and peace are all illusions in pairs.

Then we, in these new people, will no longer involve ourself in ecology movements on earth. The more people do this, the more is the environment destroyed because environmental and other movements are actions of an individual mind-set based on the premise that humans and the environment are separate beings independent from each other. We aren't. When we humans try to make or maintain an environment that is convenient for us, we tend to create one that becomes increasingly inconvenient for other solid-body beings. We humans regard our own individual selves and our societies as closed systems. We aren't. What is convenient for us is inconvenient for bacteria, insects, plants and animals and other human people and societies. This makes us become mutually destructive. That is no way to regard the environment. Regard everything as one rather than as separate, independent entities, and all these trends and movements disappear.

We have neither environmental destruction nor environmental protection.

The same thing is true of friendship. When two people try to be friends and worry about whether they are or not, they often fail because each of them is trying to arrange something convenient for herself or himself. Good friends don't think of their individual selves and needs. Simple synergy and resonance make them good friends. The same goes for falling in love. In the first place, falling in love is very often an illusion. Many people think they have fallen in love and get married only to separate soon afterwards even though they were supposedly madly in love. In such a case there wasn't real synergy or cosmic resonance but merely a mutual illusion of such. They mistook the feedback as love when in reality the feedback was only an individual need dressed up in the deceiving illusion of love. Feelings such as not wanting to lose the other or wanting to become one with the other or wanting the other as a partner are giveaway signs of individual-based thinking. This kind of mind-set is very weak because it has no ground. What is generally called falling in love is not real love, cosmic love.

What is cosmic love? It is cosmic self-love. The person we thought was our lover no longer looks like a lover but simply a lovable part of our own space Body, except that this part is now awake or cosmically reawakening. There are three kinds of lovers:

- Mistaken lovers are completely unawake, responding to vibrations coming from consciousnesses that are isolated, independent, self-seeking, disconnected from life;
- Ordinary lovers are parts of us that are partially awake, their physical bodies and spirits resonating in response to vibrations coming from consciousnesses that appreciate oneness and have gotten away from complete self-seeking;
- Cosmic lovers.

What does it feel like when we become cosmically one? We realize that our lover is not an "other" distinct from and independent of us, but is a reflection or mirror-image of ourselves, a part of our self, a part of our own space Body — like the nose or hand is of the human body. The mutual resonance is nothing like that in human love. It is a kind of cosmic narcissism. This kind of self-love is the only pure cosmic love. Burning yearning for another is not cosmic. That sort of thing is part of the individual world with all its unhappiness and confusion. Clear away the confusion of individualness and you have only self-love.

Even self-love goes, however, when perfect love is attained, because then there is only the feeling of oneness. There is nothing else but a clear sense of oneness. Self-love is still a stage on the way to regaining the transparent sense of oneness, the sense of fulfilled satisfaction. Cosmic self-love is the sensation experienced in those parts of our own space Body in which we are still not perfectly awake to being the whole universe but are beginning to regain that full and perfect self Consciousness. The instant that awareness is regained, the sensation is one of transparent oneness and fulfillment.

When that awareness is regained, oneness will make all war and peace disappear. To begin with, there is in real reality neither war nor its reverse, peace. Both are illusions, parts of the dreams or plays in our space Consciousness. Since life is the same everywhere in our dream universe, each living being in that dream is simply a reflection of us as space Consciousness. Where is there room for competition or fighting? There isn't. There is only harmony. When we escape from that karmic way of thinking — that we are separate individuals, independent of each other — we play our role in each part very evenly and harmoniously. Harmony is a mutually permeating holographic reflection. None of the peoples we are playing in can be at odds with each other because We, the one same self, run through all of them. There is no real division between people living in a society on this planet and those perhaps inhabiting some planet in the Andromeda Nebula. Everything and everyone in the Universe is mutually permeated by our self. This is how we will feel.

If the shift or imbalance in the surrounding space is corrected, there will be no more sickness, either. Go back upstream to the beginnings of the dream universe and there is neither sickness nor health. These two opposites are illusions in the dream. The more characters in the dream or the play concern themselves with health movements or healing, the more sickness appears. Make no mistake about that. See how sickness increases when you concentrate on health. Note the alarming increase of illness despite all the advances and developments that have been made in medicine. Modern medical science has marshalled every possible source it can to help deal with the ills of the human body — cytology, molecular pathology, immunology and various "-brionics." Healers have looked to every avenue available to us — to western medicine, to Oriental medicine, to alternative medicine, and to sources like faith, psychic power, voodo, and, in the olden days, even exorcism. All these guns have been trained on sickness and to what avail?

Is it so surprising, however? In the play, we have made up the body of the human being of organs, tissues, cells, molecules, atoms and particles. The complicated relationship between all these is staggering to think of, let alone control. An enormous number of terribly complicated laws function there, including permutations and combinations of cosmic laws. The number is even greater than astronomical! When one problem is solved, others have to be dealt with too. So interconnected is everything, that one motion sets off a chain reaction of changes. Most doctors and healers, however, satisfy themselves with pain relief or relief of immediate symptoms and problems.

Supposing, however, that we could assign one expert to each problem and that every one of these experts succeeded in solving their particular problem, finding a cure for the sickness on which they concentrated. Even if every person in the world became such an expert, we'd still be short. We would not have enough experts to do the job. We'd have an overload of work. Even with computers we'd have a blowout. The life system, the cosmic continuum, autonomy — none of these are possible objects of science or technology. They are not possible objects of medical science. The health and healing approach will ultimately go bankrupt by the twenty-first century.

We adults are so concerned about our bodies. What does this tell us? Even those of us who are so-called "healthy" cannot be carefree of our bodies. Why? Because we are conscious of our bodies being bound by laws, and the substances that make them up being bound also. So, actually we healthy adults have an un-free healthy body, an un-free cosmic body. We are hesitant, insecure and worried, forever thinking of staying healthy and not getting sick. We presume that the human body operates in accord with inevitable laws of physics, chemistry and biology and that we are not free to disregard these laws if we don't want to get sick. The feeling is definitely one of being under control of out-side forces, rather than of being able to control our body freely from space. It is a feeling of being bound and unfree, so different from that of the spontaneity and creativity of space. The feeling is the same for the mind and spirit as it is for the body, since the mind and spirit work in parallel with the bound body. We could call this state one of cosmic amnesia.

In the coming age, when we regain the memory of being space Consciousness and recover the state we were in before, what will it be like? For our spirit side there will be no boundary such as that of self that we experience now. There will be no sense of separation between us and others and our environment. Physically there will be no feeling of separation between us and our surroundings; there will be no sen-sation of being bound by various laws inside our body; we will be able to rid ourselves of impurities, rearrange any blocks that are out of plumb, and restore balance wherever needed. As we become again this horizontal-ly and vertically coordinated cosmic body, we will not even need the immune system. The immune system protects our human body from any fear of a harmful bacteria or other foreign protein from entering the body and destroying it. If there is perfect harmony within the body, no such substance will be able to survive even if it does enter, even for another purpose. Any excess or unnecessary organism will immediately be expelled.

The idea of an immune mechanism will be superfluous and no longer needed. Everything will simplify and we will be able to live under all conditions.

What happens in the meantime? Same thing. Even on this interim level of recovered Consciousness there are impurities, toxins and karma to be expelled and layers and layers of imbalance to correct. We brought numerous useless laws into being in the effort to maintain symmetry. As a result of this interference, however, we have lost the ability to manipulate our bodies freely. We can free ourselves from all this, however, and as we extricate ourselves from feeling bound by all these laws, rules and traditions we've become slaves to, and get the human bodies in which we are playing better balanced and regulated, those bodies will be movable, even unconsciously. As we recover that state there will be less and less reason for the bodies we're acting in to age or die; they should be able to be used (live on) for eternity. From the viewpoint of medical science, that is impossible. It is a dictum of medical experts that the human has a limited life span, and they even propose statistics to prove it! A limited lifespan is so in the case of human bodies made of weak or blunt cells. When we have transformed ourselves even down to the level of our cells, however, such laws will no longer apply. Eternal youth will be natural. This is not imagination or expansive delusion.

In the play, the future of humankind depends on whether a generation which is heartily convinced of the possibility of eternal youth appears or not. Most of the adult humans alive today will probably not recover, for we algo-net people are under the spell of modern scientific "common sense." Since our bodies and minds are enslaved to such thinking, we are limited in life, activity and creativity. Social organizations also are limited. In fact they are already failing. Clearly, no totally open, free, liberated people or social organizations will be born out of these conditions. The starting point will be the liberation of the self and the liberation of the human body from thinking and separateness.

It is senseless for children to continue on in the ways we adults have been going. They need to do what comes cosmically out of their bodies.

Granted, life in the twenty-first century will be a vast improvement over life as we experience it now, yet it will not be a bigger and better version of life on the same line of progress we see today. It will be on a different plane altogether. Today's science and technology are inadequate to the job of providing systems which are organic and living. They are unable, for example, to come up with interiors that respond fully to living people, like organs, tissues and cells respond to each other, nor can they come up with living exteriors and structural designs. Even with the combined help of art and other forces of civilization today, they are incapable of it, because these forces are moving in the same old catalyst line — a different line, in a different direction than that in which we will be moving from here on in. Therefore, life in the twenty-first century will not be an extension of today's individualist, materialist, catalyst self and civilization.

The newspapers and TV news are full of reports about the serious efforts we humans are involved in, such as to develop health and healing, save the schools, repair the family, revive religion, and deal with the revolting young people. Following these news sources certainly does give you the impression that at least 99% of the population is still locked into the catalyst play, totally unaware of the paradigm shift now going on. Where are the people who are even partially waking up?

You'd think we could find them among the professional religious people who are supposed to be detached from the world enough to recognize the nature of momentous changes. But no.

How about the meditators, the searchers, the modern gurus and followers of the updated versions of traditional religions and philosophies such as Zen, Yoga and American Indian, the hip metaphysicians who write of consciousness, the healers and the natural health prophets, the macrobiotic and natural hygiene nutritionists, and the astonishing number of channellers and psychics who purport to give us an inner track to the unknown? Are they the new people or just the last act of this play? Obviously the last act of this play.

Where do you find the new people, the new consciousness?

Surprisingly, many of them are among the pop musicians, artists and writers of the world. You also find them among certain people who on the outside look like very straight people but upon closer look are surprisingly awakened. There are even a few rare scientists whose creative, open minds free them from the algo-net. More than any others, however, the ones to look to for evidence of the new life coming back into play would be the children.

There are many examples of such "new children" everywhere today, but the experiences of two families here in Japan illustrate the point well. The mothers of both families had been at their wits ends as to how they could deal with their rebellious youngsters. The children either refused to go to school and/or behaved very roughly. They were very strong both physically and in character. Neither threats nor discipline phased them.

The copious advice of books and professionals on this widespread modern behavioral phenomenon failed to help them, so both asked for advice. It wasn't necessary to quote the enlightened experts of catalyst society: "Yes, that's difficult! Are you giving them attention instead of being out all the time trying to make money?" It wasn't necessary to repeat the list of last-hope approaches such as "More discipline! Firmer control! Cane them in public! Build more prisons to lock them up in." In fact it was not necessary to think at all.

It was immediately apparent that these children were new beings of a new world dawning, and that the problem was not the children but rather the mothers. The children were frustrated, having to resist the imposition of what they deeply felt were mortally stifling rules, ideas and ways. No amount of time or discipline would improve the situation. Instead the mothers would have to change. They could rectify the situation if they themselves changed, if they dropped all their adult values, if they stopped trying to teach the children and instead let go and trusted that everything about their childrens' upbringing would be working out fine, autonomously.

To their great credit, they did change. It took great courage for them to drop demands that they had always believed would help their children grow up into successful, happy people. It took great courage to try this new way instead of sticking to the firm discipline approach and enduring the trouble and conflict it usually entails until the child eventually sees the light.

These mothers made 180 degree turns. No rules. The children could do whatever they really wanted to do. And that held for everything — when they slept, when they got up, when they ate, what they ate, what they did with their time. No preaching to them on values, no judgments about whether the childrens' decisions were good or bad, enlightened or stupid, dangerous or safe. One of the children refused to go to school. Another one wanted to go to school — but to play with friends, not to learn. She refused to do the lessons or be taught. Every day she has to stand in the corner.

Besides that, however, the mothers joined the children. Both mothers and children sleep when they feel sleepy. They get up when they feel like it. They eat whenever they feet hungry. No more twenty-four-hour days with three meals (morning, noon and night), and to bed on time and up early. (And they have husbands too, but that is another story.)

What happened? Their children's obnoxious behavior stopped. Communication opened up between them. One of the children, a boy of only six, even explained consciously the reason for his stance. He sat bolt upright one night when they were sleeping and said to his mother: "Do you want to know why I didn't want to go to school? I wonder if you can follow this." The mother gulped, wondering what sort of story he might have about UFOs or something. "If I have to learn 1+1=2, and that sort of rule, I will lose my power. Can you understand?" His mother hesitantly nodded that she sort of did.

Later, she asked me what it meant. Well, math and the laws of physics and what we call the laws of nature (being bound by gravity, etc.) apply only to an extremely small part of the universe. The vast majority of the universe exists and operates without any law. But most of our scientists and teachers do not know this; it is not part of their consciousness. So they go on teaching that we have no alternative but to accept living under the limitations of laws and are best off if we know what they are and how to manage most effectively under them — in other words, go to school and learn.

The boy went to school for a short time and soon realized what they were going to do to him. He would be taught over and over that these laws apply to everything. They would have a law for everything he would think or do, and get him used to first learning the endless laws and then following them. Eventually he would be conditioned to thinking that way himself.

At first he went along with it as sort of a game, knowing in his heart that it was not true. But he could see that before long he would come under the spell of this mentality. He would get used to thinking that he had to follow some formula, rule or law in order to figure things out or act. But he already knew that this was unnecessary, so why subject himself to it. The teachers and the school, however, were strict about it. He soon began to feel that it was not going to be a game with them. That is why he didn't want to go to school any more. He didn't want to be tied into the human system because he was aware of a much easier, more effective system he was already at home in — that of space Consciousness. He didn't want to lose that freedom and power. He was resisting efforts to force him out of that world into the human play world.

There are more examples of new consciousness, signs of it in ordinary children, documented in several TV documentaries in Japan — children who can read through their hands and ears and feet. Recently, story after story has appeared of children telling of extraordinary things once their parents changed, stopped enforcing adult values and rules on them, believed in them and began to resonate with them. There are similar stories of children in China, America and Russia as well.

We are going to deal with this more at length in a later book, but even from this simple introduction we can get a clue as to the way this transition from human consciousness back to space Consciousness is going to take place: First parents, teachers and other authorities will stop enforcing traditional adult human catalyst values and rules. Then the children and parents will begin to resonate, the children will begin to communicate, and the parents too will regain their powers of space Consciousness.

If we don't enforce discipline on our young aren't we going to have a big mess on our hands? Won't the world become one big graffito, or even worse, one big blown up junkyard or graveyard? We will see things differently if we view this behavior as cosmic frustration being exhibited so that we notice something new is up. If we courageously defuse their frustration and if we go beyond that and join them in their concern for a new consciousness to rule the behavior of life, we may find them letting us in on their consciousness. They may be unconscious of what it is that makes them unwilling to accept adult values, or they may be clear about it, like the boy described above. At any rate, we will not have a mess on our hands if we respond and resonate to the new consciousness of our children, because mess is only an adult value judgment made from an algo-net point of view. On the contrary. We will have a mess on our hands if we don't listen to them, for few of us have that space Consciousness of what is in the making.

As the great Producer/Director of the Earth Story, we have decided that the goal of all characters in the drama of life from now on will be to return to the original state — from the world of thought to the world of no-thought, from the world of being a human (or whatever), to the world of beings with full Consciousness, in one great leap. I say great because a 100% return to our full Consciousness involves a correcting or rebalancing of the whole gamut of evolved beings we are playing and performing in — the sun, the planets, the planet Earth, animals, plants and bacteria, atoms and particles — in a few human pieces of the universe hologram.

We are already entering an era of play in which we will have very ordinary people, under very ordinary circumstances using our space Consciousness rather than science and technology. It will be an era of uncivilized children — awake beings who don't think at all. There will be no so-called adults, nor children who have been brought up and trained by adults.

This will be very hard for those of us with education and training to accept, no doubt, and for those of us with typical adult feelings. That is the way it will be, however, because the civilized ways that characterized us catalyst humans are to give way to new ways of intuition and connectedness. This is not to insinuate disrespect for everyone and everything, but an appreciation for the possibilities of new life on the planet and in the cosmos because of our connectedness. Don't think, just do. Do and experience and know with full Conscious-ness of who you are and your connectedness to all.

Children intuitively know that the twenty-first century will come out of a different dimension than present-day civilization, so they say things like: "What adults are now doing is only for the time being." To put it simply, the twenty-first century will grow naturally and spontaneously out of the inside of the body. By that I mean that whatever we do will happen naturally, spontaneously. As I mentioned earlier, when playing with computers something comes out of children that doesn't come out of adults who use the same computer and who originally created both the hardware and software the children are using. It is as though the children are coming out of a different space. They are already future cosmic beings not confined in the same imaginary play world to which we present-day earth humans feel bound. They are refusing to conform to present-day adult earth life because they are already internally oriented, most of them still unconsciously, to what is going to be standard and normal in the next stage of the dream or play.

We have decided that it is senseless, therefore, to have the children continue on in the ways we've had the adults going in. They need to and will do what comes cosmically out of their bodies — which are linked to the Universe in a live way, as live-net beings in a world of true, honest feelings. They and their lives will be a new extension of the life system of our Universe Body/Mind, very different than that of the present catalyst adult mind and body set. It follows, therefore, that their lifestyle will be totally different. So will the way they design the tools they use. Types of information will change. The bases of life will be different. What replaces catalyst human relationships and social organization will be totally different. Principles will be different.

We already have the children evolving this way today. They have started evolving from the inside and operate with fuller consciousness. Their inside is different than the inside of adults in that it contains a higher proportion of ectoplasm. All the more reason why adults don't understand them. What the children of the future are trying to be and what kind of society they are in the process of making cannot be read from the viewpoint of present-day human adults. It cannot be surmised from surveys, polls and analyses of trends, directions and what people are doing now.

In short, children are trying to live (many of them unconsciously) in an ontologocal way, as cosmic beings not as humans — to live without thinking, to do everything without laboring under the burden of limitations created by thinking-human catalyst authorities, to provoke a chain reaction among cosmic laws. Like them, we adults should rely solely on the power of our space Consciousness — which is our own real self. In our space Consciousness is the power to omnisciently and omnipotently rearrange the order of things without thinking. We suddenly realize it is we who as space Consciousness create the play. So if we switch our minds and take the standpoint of ourself as the Dreamer, or the Player, we realize that we can do whatever we want, without a lot of thinking about how to do it. It is so easy to rearrange the substances inside any body, to rearrange them down to even the tiniest most elementary particles in our human bodies, if we use full Consciousness and not just the partial, amnesic consciousness we have used while playing the part of so-and-so, human being. This is so much better than to grunt and groan like the ascetics of ancient times; so much easier than taking the time and trouble to cast the demons out of ourselves. While we are just floating, the inside of our human body is all rearranged and transformed from its former human-ness to something cosmically renewed.

There are already some children with chakras open, living this life of no-thinking as the Dreamer, space Consciousness. There is a danger that if they are taught by adults who will naturally and with all good intentions brainwash them with traditional algo-net adult values and laws, they will be spoiled, harmed and broken. The only way the children can avoid this is to be maintained as authentic cosmic beings, not to be trained or disciplined by adults; and even if they have to go to school, to maintain a deaf ear and a closed mind to algo-net education. If they don't do this, they are finished. It's all right for them to look like they are cooperating, but they have no choice but to reject it.

There is no other way. Look at children carefully. The more sensitive the child, the less likely that it will willingly receive or accept guidance from today's algo-net adults. Those children who refuse to go along with algo-net adult upbringing are the ones who are moving in the direction of natural evolution as holograms of the universe. We should learn from and follow them.

What are the values of the algo-net adult humans? Look at the various cultures and civilizations of the world so far. In them we see the expressions and embodiment of the numerous human values — all of them one hundred percent deluded. We as catalysts have developed and come to cherish as valuable an unbelievable number of systems. Some are personal, some social; some abstract, some concrete; they differ from place to place. We consider many to be absolute, unquestioned values: family, religion, health, pleasure, individualism, human rights, private property, capitalism, security, having a job, having money, being loved, thinking, studying, having a college or university education and degree, having a title or important position. The list is endless, and we are under great pressure to possess and maintain all these things that are considered values in human play.

Imagine what relief it would bring to be able to say, "I want to do this particular thing no matter what anybody thinks!" Well, there is nobody else to think well or ill of us, so what is holding us back? Children are not under this burden of worrying about what others think until adults get to working on them and make sure they too are put under (and forced to endure) the rules of the game. We as space Consciousness are saying to our self now: "Let's call an end to the game." The loaf is baked to its intended size. Time to start on something new now.

Since the catalyst play or dream is to end soon, we will have the children of the next generation live without the benefit of the value systems we adults, their ancestors, devised. For them, all delusions will be dropped. A live-net future is now clearly in the works. We as space Consciousness got too wrapped up in our game of whirlpools and so involved in playing the parts of the various thinking-humans that we forgot the living network of all thought-forms in our space Body/Mind. This resulted in imbalanced, dulled or weakened cells and material (matter) systems that evolved out of them, impoverished and handicapped by their habit of slow and imperfect thinking. We could not show our true self when we were working with such a severely handicapped autonomy. As we change the situation and recover our full Consciousness and hence our perfectly balanced and coordinated autonomy, we will display our true colors again — our identity as a cosmic living network.

In the transition period, our living network will still be somewhat human, enveloped in the thick fog of thinking. Even in the children we are living in and playing in, traces and elements of old algo-net thinking habits, traditions and conditioning are still there to be found in the atoms and cells of body and mind. Even in them we are still a clouded, confused cosmic being. We will get the fog cleared, however, the tower of blocks straightened out. In the process of adjusting and correcting, dusting or scraping off the layers of darkness-producing thought, we will be reviving the vibrant living network. During the transition period to the twenty-first century, we will let it begin to dawn on all the human characters in our imagination that a profound change is taking place. Everyone will wake up to what is going on. If we human characters have eyes to see, we realize the change is already progressing rapidly.

We are already recovering at least partial awareness that we are space Consciousness only thinking up or imagining humans and other such characters rather than really giving them existence as separate, individual human beings. This light dawning on us may be only a dim, weak flicker of awareness, but it will gradually brighten, intensify and strengthen. Gradually a view of the live-net will come into sharper focus. We will see with greater clarity the many layers and stages, acts and scenes of the infinite dream and drama of life playing out in the theater of our mind — space Consciousness. Like children, very naturally we will see it, hear it, feel it and experience it. All we have to do in us still existing adult humans is stop thinking and let things happen!

GOING **B**ACK ON COSMIC CRUISE **C**ONTROL

Most of the mental and spiritual realities we humans seek are as much illusions as material reality.

After reading a book about a richer level of consciousness, our first desire as thinking-humans is naturally to have a summary or list telling us exactly how we can achieve it: Ten Steps to Higher Consciousness. The "algo-" in us loves the familiar pattern of taking procedures to solve a problem. The thinker in us wants to say, "Okay, here is a goal. Now, what do we do to achieve it?" We would like a formula to follow, preferably one that applies to everyone. We go for marketing promises, outlining all the benefits to be easily derived from following this new path. We would especially like a "Life of Yamate" on which to base our own behavior — a concrete example of how to make this extraordinary transformation take place. We are anxious to do something, and try like mad.

Hopefully, after reading this book, however, we have become aware that no amount of doing or trying, steps or study, classes, exercises or programs, intellectualizing, meditating, fasting, penance and the like are going to help us one iota toward the goal. Falling back on these would simply illustrate all the more that we have not awakened to the fact that we are not that kind of being. We are not really a separate, individual, material being. Therefore, nothing we do on our own as separate, individual humans will move us to full Consciousness. Taking steps and engaging ourselves in activities are acts we played as humans in the dream play, in a role that was meant to be. Now that catalyst role is coming to an end.

This book, therefore, has not been another analysis of the economy, the schools, the family, government, religion and medicine — our concrete human societal problems — and a program of concrete human plans to deal with them. Nor has it been another self-improvement book with a suggested outline of steps we should take to be a better human, more conscious or more spiritual, a "How To Be Enlightened" or "How To Achieve Union with God." Though written in words, this was not information for our head, a communication to us as human. It was a communication to our real self from our real self, to ourselves as space Consciousness, from ourselves as space Consciousness. It was a telepathic prompting to realize the fact that in our human role we might begin to feel new types of impulses, and, when we do, help to recognize these impulses for what they are and to recover. It has been a form of talking to our self.

If you are reading this, you are really reading to yourself. In writing this I was writing to myself, telling myself, "Wake up! Let go! Return to the simple flow of space Consciousness which is operating all the characters (organs, cells, systems) in the 'space Body', by a sort of 'cosmic autonomic nervous system'!"

If we think that study and exercises and classes and eating certain foods and praying in certain positions are going to turn us into a saint or a god, we are still not getting the point. Our consciousness has not changed. All of these are a sure giveaway that we are still using our head and that we still think we are real as a separate, individual body. What can we do, for we truly want to recover full Consciousness?

The desire to recover is the impulse I spoke of. Our response to this impulse, however, must not be to do something, or try like mad. Rather, just the opposite. We need to stop doing what we have been doing as catalysts. Reprogram our usual human responses to zero —

zero response. Awake to the fact that we are nobody and nothing. If we resonate with any of what's been pointed out in the previous chapters we will find ourselves spontaneously beginning to put a brake on this human thinking so that we can catch the telepathy, intuitive messages and inspiration coming from our real self.

When we feel like thinking something out, say "No, I'm not going to give a moment's thought to this. I'll just keep my mind still and see what happens."

When we feel like planning, say, I'm going to stop making out an agenda for getting things done successfully. No more saying for example that I have to go to college to get a good job in order to make a good living, or that my child has to. I'm not going to plan out my year. I'll just travel when I get the clear idea to, or visit so-and-so only when I really want to. I'm not going to set goals, but rather leave things up to life and see what happens. I'm not even going to plan out a daily schedule. I will stop lining up so many things to do, people to meet, and filling my schedule with a tiring round of endless expectations to meet. All of these things were part of the catalyst play. They are no longer necesssary. It is okay now to avoid getting wrapped up in them, even to protect myself. I will let go, let them go their way without my involvement. I won't let them be real.

Say, I'm going to resist the impulse to expect rituals, prayers, sacrifices, teas, magic potions, pills, herbs, incantations, priests, shamans, channellers, doctors, lawyers, therapists, books, tapes, programs and lotteries, to get me what I want. I'm going to look to myself. I'm going to rely only on our self. I'm going to take it easy, be more spontaneous, and not think about all the do's and don'ts that constantly surround me. I'm going to stop trying to control everything to work out as I have figured in my human head would be good for me. I can free myself from the whole health thing by using my space Consciousness to avoid buying into the drama that creates sickness and perpetuates it.

We can, for example, quit reading the newspapers. Stop watching TV news and talk shows — "must" pastimes that keep us all worked up and involved in the dramas of old catalyst life. Many of us can quit working. It becomes very easy if we see through the classic triple catalyst incentive ruse — the obsession with making money, becoming important or securing power that drives us to so much effort. Refuse catalyst jobs and activities that are stressful, unpleasant and not what we really want to be doing. Drop out of the present school system and the whole process of indoctrination in catalyst human thoughts and ways. Stop going to church. Get away from channelling and the fascination with tangible experiences of the paranormal which are no more important for us than bodily experiences since they are only on the level of energy body. Decline participation in all movements and protests — peace, health and environmental — as though the world were real or as though we could possibly understand the whole picture that space Consciousness has in mind.

Change the subject of conversations or begin shying away from even talking about politics and politicians, problems of economy, jobs, taxes, corruption, crafty lawyers, ripoff carpenters, mechanics, plumbers, electricians and other service people, the sad state of the nation and the world, rising medical costs and a hopelessly imbalanced criminal justice system based on laws and methods that even sensible people are beginning to call games and dumb. Throw off all limitations on our movements. None of these are real. They are figments of our imagination — our imagination as space Consciousness. They were a play that we made up in our mind.

Say over and over: This situation, good or bad, is of my own making. That boss or worker who just irritated me again is Me ! That person who just said something I don't like is Me. Why would I do this to myself, put myself in such a situation, or say this to myself? To wake Me up. To keep Me honest. To balance Myself.

Sleep as much as possible. Don't say I've got to get up and get this and that done. Take it easy. Refuse to be rushed, overscheduled, imposed on. We needn't rush our self. Give plenty of time to do each thing we want to do. We feel we have to take part in this or that? No we don't. This and that are of no real consequence to us anymore. Time to end the catalyst play. Try it once and you'll see.

We will be considered dropouts, wierdos; we will be criticized for being irresponsible, unwilling to be involved, cold, unpatriotic, godless. But just try it once and we see how much smoother things go. We really take a load off our minds. We feel liberated. We relax. We calm down. We begin to feel so much better. Thanks to this new awareness we rise above fear, no longer feel anxiety, jealousy or anger. What new awareness? The awareness or consciousness that as a human we are only a make-believe character, an illusion we created in our own mind. The awareness that all we see is of our own making. That is ME. That is My creation. The awareness that we are space Consciousness. How do we get this awareness back? By wiping out the old one! Ditch what's in our mind now. Reduce the whole content of our present mind-set to zero and start over fresh. Namely, turn off any thinking such as: I am Jane, or John. I am a solid material body. I have a family and friends. I possess this and that. I need money. I have such and such sickness. I will get old and die. I believe in God who will reward or punish me. The list is endless, depending on how much indoctrination we have been exposed to.

It is all just a matter of consciousness. If we don't give those things reality in our mind, they don't exist.

We can start now to eliminate the whole catalyst play from our mind, from our consciousness.

Changing our viewpoint does the trick. Instead of viewing ourselves as human so-and-so, see ourself as pure Consciousness. What are we thinking up? What are we imagining in our consciousness? Let's say, for example, in our mind we have been making up a body, a human body. We see it in our mind. We see several bodies — different sizes and shapes. We have had them living in a house. They drive a car. We put a cat and trees in the yard. We have one of the characters who is a male go to an office building where he meets other people like him. They have meetings or they make things. There is a female who takes little copies of herself off to a school, then she goes to a building where she meets other people like herself. They are putting together a magazine which all the characters who look like human people, read for information or pleasure. They stop from time to time to drink coffee. They drink through mouths in the front of the part of their body, which is called a head, with a face on it. The coffee is made from beans which are grown on plants in some other countries which are situated on a planet called earth which is revolving around a sun together with several other planets.

On and on the imagining goes. It is infinite in detail. We have thousands of stories going on at the same time. There are sights, sounds, aromas, tastes and feelings in these stories. In other stories there are no bodies. Invisible spirits interact.

If we want to, we can make a character or event disappear by simply getting it out of our mind, out of our consciousness. We can change the whole story or the whole drift of things. Nothing is in our consciousness unless we make it up in the first place and allow it to stay after it is there. Everything is literally all in our head. Everything is a matter of consciousness — what we choose to imagine, ponder, or allow in our mind.

We think that things go on existing and moving even if we are not consciously thinking about them. No. Even our limited human consciousness is part of the whole Consciousness. Full Consciousness is our consciousness, not someone else's — someone off in the clouds.

Isn't this dangerous? Doesn't it lead to our getting out of touch with the real world? Isn't that schizophrenia, a serious mental psychotic state? No. Psychosis, doctors, hospitals, and all these other beings, events and happenings are themselves only imagined beings, events or happenings. There is no other real world, only our pure Consciousness. Those who think they are the reality are the ones who are deluded and who often become mentally sick because of being confused between imagination and real reality which is pure Consciousness.

Try it, you'll see. Far from damaging ourselves, we find ourselves liberated, alive, empowered. If we know we are the only real being, we have no sense of dichotomy, no sense of split. We find all fears, all worries, all anxieties, complexes, strains and stresses reduced to nothing.

We say to ourself: There is only Me and I am pure consciousness. All else is My imagination, illusion caused by the flow of My stream of consciousness.

We can then abandon ourselves and completely entrust ourselves to our space Consciousness enveloping and sustaining us. We let our real self take over and do the work. This is the way of no thinking.

As human, the best model we can imagine is a tiny fetus or infant: no thoughts, no words, no concerns for whether its parents are rich or poor, powerful or helpless, brilliant or slow, strong or sickly, admired or rejected. Just there, conscious and alive, trusting and open. This attitude of the fetus is like our leaving the operation of our organs and bodily systems completely and trustingly to the working of our autonomic nervous system. The cosmos, our space body has its own autonomic nervous system.

Cosmic energy operates and moves us through our ectoplasm. Our breathing, the operation of our organs, glands, digestion, elimination, all are operated by our ectoplasm. (Remember, ectoplasm is a phenomenon. So it doesn't exist as such. It is an ontological being.) We don't have to consciously do anything for these organs and systems to work in perfect order and balance. Just avoid screwing them up by putting toxins into the system — eg., bad food, bad air, etc. — or releasing toxins into our systems from within our body — eg., toxic substances released from glands when we are under stress, worried, or angry and frustrated.

When we return to zero (when we feel nothing can be done, when we're at our wits end, when we say "I'm finished!"), then our real self, our full Consciousness, can manipulate us, because we give up our limited control; we relinquish command of our ship, we get our oar out of the water and just abandon ourselves. Then things really BOOM! They go smoothly (like our flow of blood, our liver and other organs, tissues, cells and atoms really operate smoothly when in balance under the direction of our autonomic nervous system).

At times like this we say: "Anything is all right. Go with the flow. Let it be, let it be. Its fine with me." As long as we insist on following the thoughts, plans and goals we entertain as human players, however, we have mostly trouble. What we do is not as smooth and successful as it could be.

Ordinarily, however, it is hard for us humans to believe that. We keep wanting to interfere, to meddle, to monkey around, to keep our hand in things. Like a manager who can't delegate authority, we keep wanting to do everything ourselves, watch each move. Or we go to the other extreme and leave everything to others — a god, a doctor, the politicians. There are no others. There is only our real self.

One other thing that we especially need to let go of is the idea of cause and effect. We tend as humans to do everything with this mentality. We presume we have to have a cause for every effect. So when anything happens, we immediately ask "Why did that happen?"

For example, when we have heartburn, we ask, "What did I eat?"

This is simple. But other things are more complex. We couldn't get at the cause if we studied it a million years. Yet we try, and often we think we have the answer. Better to ignore it — just look at it and leave it to our space Body and space mind. Let it be, whatever it is. It will work out all right. We don't need to figure out why and come up with a solution. Our solutions might be all wrong or just wrong enough to move things off in another direction that would mess up other things and make matters worse. Resist the impulse to cause/effect thinking.

• Don't think, for example, I should be healthy because I am eating healthy food, or because I'm exercising. By the same token, don't eat certain foods and do exercise because it will make you healthy.
• Don't write in order to sell, to entertain, or to change the world.

• Don't meditate in order to advance or become enlightened, or recover consciousness.

Give up all such planning. Do nothing rather than do something with a meaning, with a goal, thinking our action will cause an important effect. Do everything as play, as meaningless fun, not as a cause of some effect to come about as a result of our doing it. Even saying I'm doing nothing in order to achieve enlightenment is clearly performing an act with the thought of it being a cause to produce an effect. Since we are space Consciousness, just dreaming a thing up gives it existence. There is no process necessary. Process and such laws as cause and effect are only elements of the play we have dreamed up. They are not a part of our world as Consciousness. So it is foolish to feel bound by those laws that are working only in our mind.

What do we do then? Give up. Just watch. Feel for the flow — let our feelers out to sense or intuit the flow, catch the telepathy.

Let our space Body do its thing because our individual solid body is the illusion being played out in and by our Consciousness. Leave everything to our space Consciousness. The cells inside our body do not have to know how the body is going to take care of itself. They just let go and leave it all to the autonomic nervous system. Space Consciousness is our cosmic autonomic nervous system. Go on cosmic cruise control; set the controls on automatic pilot, and sit back to enjoy the trip.

We know we can't operate our liver or our kidneys, or our sensing systems. We accept that and just let them do their thing. We know that all we have to do is avoid throwing blocks in their way — bad food, stress and anger poisons. We have to leave everything to their autonomous operation. They work fine without our help, without our interference, without our meddling. If we meddle — like when we start monkeying around with pills and procedures, upsetting the balance of hormones and the immune system — we can get things pretty messed up, even though temporarily we feel better or think our condition is improved.

Better to let go, leave all to our space Consciousness which is our cosmic autonomic nervous system. Then we see how smoothly things go!

Our catalyst job is over, so now we don't have to get up and get going. When we do, however, it will be because our space Consciousness is getting us up. All we have to do is just let go and be like a fetus. Let ourselves be operated, informed with this spirit, free to move in whatever direction we go. No controlling, no pleading, no thinking up, planning, figuring out reasons why, or how to solve what seem like problems. Go with the flow.

Too many of us have spent too much time studying consciousness and spiritual life, too much time trying to advance or achieve spiritual goals on our own. Enlightenment … Union with God… Love… Harmony… Most of the mental and spiritual realities we humans seek are as much illusions as material reality. Full Consciousness cannot be reached through the human mind or body or through human methods. Nor can it be reached through the energy body and the methods of channelling and so forth. In fact, none are necessary. There is no other to reach or become. We already are what as humans we want to become. Even with limited consciousness we are the one same Consciousness. We are all there is. We can only wake up to it, become sensitive to it and experience it going on in ourselves. As humans we will wake up to it when our space Consciousness wants to. All we have to do is wait patiently, accepting our role.

We can take moments out each day to reconnect with and to experience our real self. How? Just consciously open up to let our whole being listen, look, and feel. Pay attention to what we notice, whether it seems inside or outside of us. Don't try to understand what we experience. Refrain from trying to organize it or expand it, control or operate it. Without straining, open out our whole being. It will take time to become sensitive to our home world of non-thinking again. That world is there, even if we aren't aware. As we become sensitive again, however, we will become aware of it also.

The way of ontology is like a nothingness exercise in which we return to our center (which is materially zero, nothing). It is simple way. It is a way of no thinking. Relax. Take it easy. Consciously recall that in this bag of skin we are just a costumed character in a play routine we started out to enjoy. Everything else around us is just that also. It's all a part of a play. Our own play. Nothing so important. Foolish matter to be sucked into seriously. We take off our costume and make-up for a bit. We open up our whole being. Detach from and let go completely of all the others that appear to be so important (people, positions, responsibilities and goals). Like a tiny blood cell we are floating around inside the enveloping, sustaining body of the universe. The cosmic autonomic nervous system is capable of taking care of running everything perfectly. We abandon ourselves, entrust ourselves to the flow. Don't think, don't imagine, don't judge, don't analyze. Just watch … listen … feel … resonate … grasp … intuit … recover this Consciousness:

)

All this is illusion:
Me, in this human form. Family and friends. Cities and
   countries. Activities and job. The bad and the beautiful.

The corrupt and the sincere. Successes and failures. Fears and certitudes. All this oh-so-important stuff that weighs so heavily: traditions, rules and law; a thousand dos and don'ts. Pressures and stress. Visas, taxes, threats and insurance. Sickness, old age, retirement and death. Bills and debt, crime, violence and corruption. But as well, the pleasantries of poetry, honor, fidelity, loyalty and love. The pleasures of body, mind and spirt — sex and sport, scholarship, music, art, and food.

I the human am just one among billions of shapes and forms of whirling energy, thought waves — nothing but a pebble, a chip of wood, an insect. Hardly to be taken so seriously. I am a clever, complicated illusion. All the other beings and activities around me are that also — nothing else. I can leave all this play to my cosmic autonomic nervous system.

Behind all this play is the real Me.

The way of no thinking has allowed Me to wake up.

I am the only really existing being.

All else is illusion. Only shapes and dreams unreally existing in My Consciousness.

All is well.

The Universe is My thought, My game, My dream.

I am the dreamer of the Universe, the dreamer of everything and nothing. I will go on playing and dreaming forever. Even now I am making up new games and dreaming new dreams.

I am everything and everything is nothing — this is reality.

The only reality is Me.

The real me is pure Consciousness.

I am infinite, unembodied Consciousness with a head full of
dreams.

Afterword

What can you the reader do to pursue this awakening you have received from this contact with Yamate? Nothing! The fact is, you already are awakening, or else you would not have read all the way through this book.

Yamate-san has no concrete programs to involve those who are attracted to his ideas and want to join him in space consciousness. Aware, however, that we share the burden of having forgotten who we really are, he accedes to the inquiries of those who are experiencing this common impulse to awaken by suggesting how they might simulate the state of space Consciousness.

On Saturday evenings in a small rented room above a public bath in Tokyo, he holds special sessions. He begins with a short talk to those who come. The talk usually consists of observations about roadblocks to recovery and encouragement to detach from human ideals and values in which we have become too absorbed.

The short talk is followed by a long period in which Yamate-san guides everyone in a simulation of the transition from limited human consciousness to space consciousness. He calls this transition *meiso*. At first we hear him describing his consciousness expanding from the everyday, limited sensations of sight, sound and feeling experienced through his senses, to an experience of his entire being. He descends back through his skin inside his body, down through his organs, deeper into the cells which make up the organs, then down to molecules, atoms, and particles, back to nothingness. In this state of nothingness, he is free of any name, any title, any relationships, any possessions, free of the tyranny of every value, rule and law. He remains in this state, letting it take over and permeate his human consciousness as an habitual, renewed mind-set, making him receptive to the inflow of full space consciousness.

Like a flight simulator, *meiso* simulates our awakening into full consciousness, beginning with a return to nothingness or zero. It is not a system or practice. According to Yamate, making a system or program out of *meiso* in order to try and bring about an awakening would actually hinder us from awakening. We humans are prone to want to do something to cause an effect, but that's not how the awakening happens. In fact, it is not as humans that we recover at all. We are actually the full, real self that is recovering from being human. The *meiso* simulation will be a dead end if we perform it under the imbalanced direction of human consciousness in the spirit of "Think, use your head, figure out what you are doing and what your goal is. Refine and refine the goal (which makes it more complicated and difficult), concentrate like mad, try hard and endure all hardships (which are numerous and almost overwhelming)."

Instead, we simulate *meiso* when we relax, simply focus our attention on the outside of our bodies, then see our whole being opening up and abandon ourselves completely. We entrust ourselves to that which is all around us, vitally connected to us, and omnipotent and omniscient. In this state, we simply watch, listen, feel, intuit. We gradually become conscious of many things. What comes to us differs from person to person and time to time. Many times all is just silence.

We don't have to go to Tokyo to experience *meiso*, nor do we have to travel to a sacred or "energy" place, or even to a place of quiet, though we usually like to begin in a place where we can relax completely. We can all experience *meiso* at any time, in any place, standing, sitting, watching TV, or sleeping. It begins simply with a simulation of a state of nothingness, in which all the thoughts, values, concerns, hang-ups, and plans we have as humans have been reduced to zero.

We can experience *meiso* for one minute or one hour, or find that we are eventually experiencing it for longer periods of time until it has become a habitual mind-set, a continuous state of consciousness. In this state we wait patiently, like a baby in a crib, as our space Consciousness fully awakens within us.

—*Robert Engler and Yuriko Hayashi*